Believe

Boxing, the Olympics and My Life Outside the Ring

NICOLA ADAMS WITH
JORDAN PARAMOR

PENGUIN BOOKS

PENGUIN BOOKS

UK | USA | Canada | Ireland | Australia
India | New Zealand | South Africa

Penguin Books is part of the Penguin Random House group of companies
whose addresses can be found at global.penguinrandomhouse.com.

First published by Viking 2017
Updated edition published with two new chapters in Penguin Books 2018

001

Copyright © Nicola Adams and Jordan Paramor, 2017, 2018

The moral right of the author has been asserted

Set in 12.96/15.6 pt Garamond MT Std
Typeset by Jouve (UK), Milton Keynes
Printed and bound in Great Britain by Clays Ltd, Elcograf S.p.A.

A CIP catalogue record for this book is available from the British Library

ISBN: 978-0-241-98055-2

www.greenpenguin.co.uk

MIX
Paper from
responsible sources
FSC® C018179

Penguin Random House is committed to a
sustainable future for our business, our readers
and our planet. This book is made from Forest
Stewardship Council® certified paper.

PENGUIN BOOKS
BELIEVE

Nicola Adams OBE is the reigning Olympic, World, Commonwealth Games and European Games boxing champion at flyweight. She became the first woman in the UK to win an Olympic Gold medal for boxing during London 2012 and won her second Olympic Gold in Rio 2016. She topped the list of the *Independent*'s 101 most influential LGBT people in Britain for 2012 and was voted *Glamour*'s Sportswoman of the Year in 2013. She has also appeared as an extra in *Coronation Street* and *Emmerdale*, and had a cameo appearance in the BBC drama series *Waterloo Road*, where she played herself.

Prologue

'And the winner is . . .'

As I raised my fist into the air and listened to the crowd screaming my name, I knew my life would never be the same again. I had just beaten my arch-rival Ren Cancan in the London Olympics and become the first woman ever to win an Olympic gold medal for boxing. I'd made history and it felt incredible.

I'd like to say what happened on 9 August 2012 came as a big surprise to me, but I'd be lying. I've known since I was thirteen years old that, one day, I would be standing in a boxing ring having just made history.

I may have come up against a lot of adversity and been challenged with some serious injuries along the way but I always knew I'd make it somehow. I had the determination, the skills and the focus. And most importantly, I believed I would.

One:

The Warm-up

If you'd told me when I was eleven years old that I'd become a world-champion boxer one day, I would have laughed at you. At that age I was more interested in climbing trees and winding up my brother, Kurtis. I was just a normal kid who went on to have very big dreams.

I was born at St James's Hospital in Leeds at 7.20 a.m. on 26 October 1982. I weighed in at 7lb 12oz, which, considering I'm now only 5 foot 4, is pretty sturdy.

I was a real mummy's girl when I was very young, and I still am, but my mum is the only person in the world who's allowed to call me that. I didn't like anyone apart from her holding me and I used to go mad if anyone else tried to pick me up. I also cried a lot, which seems weird, because I'm really not a crier at all these days. It takes a lot to get me emotional.

My mum, Dee, said I was a happy baby and a mischievous toddler and always getting into some kind of bother. And while I may have cried a lot, I also smiled a lot, which is something that's continued to this day. People often comment on the fact that I'm always smiling and, because I was so cheerful, my mum signed me up with a local modelling agency and I started doing some jobs

3

here and there. I didn't do it for very long because my parents were both working and I was being asked to go to Scotland for shoots and all sorts and it became really hard work getting me from place to place.

I began to suffer very badly from eczema as a young child so my mum was always worrying about me. Once, when I was tiny, she left me in my cot to run downstairs and get something and when she came back I'd scratched my arms so badly they wouldn't stop bleeding and she had to take me to hospital to get checked out. I'd somehow got my scratch mittens off and my skin was so raw the doctors said it looked like I had a serious burn.

I had to have cream on my skin at all times and I was so good at getting my scratch mittens off my doctor told my mum to get a pair of socks over them on my hands and attach them around my back with elastic to keep them in place. It was the only way she could be sure I could be left alone for more than five minutes without scratching myself.

I was allergic to all dairy products when I was a baby so my mum had to feed me on soya milk once I stopped breastfeeding. She tried me on formula, like most mums do, but I kept being sick and eventually they discovered that I was allergic to all sorts of things. As I got older and tried different foods things got worse, and by the time I was three I was basically allergic to life. I was allergic to nuts, fish, chocolate, dairy products . . . you name it. Thankfully, the only thing I'm still allergic to now is nuts, but my allergy is pretty severe.

Mum first found out I was allergic to nuts one Christmas when she fed me a tiny bit and I came up in this bright red stinging-nettle-type rash.

If I ate the wrong thing I was sick or went into shock. Once, I ended up in hospital after eating some chocolate. The only way my mum could find out what was wrong with me was by feeding me small amounts of foods. It was a process of elimination, and all she could do was try me out with everything and see how I'd react.

At that point, a rash or vomiting were the only side effects, but as time went on my reaction became worse, to the point where, if I ingested nuts by mistake, my throat would close up and I'd become really breathless. It was a nightmare, because my mum had to keep an eye on me at all times, and once I started nursery and then went on to school she had to let all of my teachers know about my allergies.

Of course, she also had to educate me about what I couldn't eat, so I didn't share food with the other kids. She had to make me special meals, and I used to hate eating different things to the rest of my classmates. I was probably the only kid who actually *wanted* to eat school dinners, but everything was too risky.

There came a time when I was able to eat school dinners if they were closely monitored and very simple. But even though I was grateful for this, I hated the fact that the teachers made you stay and eat it all, even if you didn't like it. They'd watch you and only let you get down when you'd finished.

One day when I was about six I had a proper stand-off with a teacher because I was given mushy peas and I hated them. I ended up sitting at the table all lunchtime because I flatly refused to eat them, so I think it's safe to say I was pretty strong-willed, even at a very young age. I sat there crying because I wanted to go and play with my friends, and in the end the teacher had to let me go because I had a class to get to, and I was so pleased, because I felt like I'd won. It may only have been a small victory but it was one of my first, and even something as silly as that gave me a buzz.

After that day, I realized that the teachers couldn't force me to eat anything I didn't like. I had the power! I got smart quickly and the teachers soon learnt that, no matter how long they made me stare at my plate of food, I wouldn't give in. I knew that if I sat there long enough I would be victorious. Once I became aware of that, I never cried about my lunch again, I just stood my ground.

I developed asthma when I was about three or four, and that was also a big worry for my mum. I remember when it started really clearly. I was in bed and I suddenly found it hard to breathe. I felt like a baby elephant was stood on my chest and my mum was really worried about me so she took me to hospital. (I was a bit of a regular at Leeds General.) They diagnosed me as having serious asthma and gave me an inhaler. They also told my mum I wouldn't be able to run around for a while, and that really upset me because I was at that age where everyone at school was playing tag and bulldog and I wasn't allowed to join in. After a couple of days of being really good and watching from the sidelines I got really bored, so I started playing with everyone again. I'm not sure it was the most sensible thing to do, but you try telling a four-year-old they can't play with their mates!

Apparently, I faked an asthma attack before school once because I didn't want to go. Mum was wise to it, though, so she sent me to school anyway. I still have an inhaler now but my asthma isn't something I ever worry about. It may not always have been the best idea to join in with the other kids' games, but I think if my mum had followed the doctor's advice and not allowed me to be active at all it could have had a big impact on me and I wouldn't have turned out to be sporty later on. I wonder if I would have been less bold if I'd believed everything I was told. These days, being asthmatic only affects me if I don't warm up my lungs properly before I train, so that's a priority. If I don't, I end up getting that sensation of breathlessness you get when you run to the top of a long flight of stairs.

I have to make sure my body is ready, and I've got a gadget that I use to exercise my lungs every morning. It makes them bigger and stronger and I can set it to different levels so it helps to increase my lung capacity.

It's like resistance training. If it's at a low level, the resistance is minimal, but I can go up levels to make it harder. It's like a workout for your lungs, I guess.

I think that everything I had to deal with early on in my childhood made me stronger and more determined as I grew up. I really do think there's some truth in that. I was never bullied or anything but I did feel different, because I was aware that I couldn't always join in with things. Children's parties were a nightmare food-wise, so I'd even have to take my own snacks along to them, which didn't feel very cool.

My mum still says now that I wasn't an 'ordinary' child. Other children smelt of baby powder and I smelt of coal-tar-solution paste. I used to have to bath in coal-tar soap to ease my eczema, and then Mum would smother me in coal-tar paste and put my clothes on over the top straight away while it was still wet so I couldn't rub it off. My skin was always so hot and sore from where I'd scratched it so much and, because the cream was cold, it was soothing, but it was also really sticky and uncomfortable. So it provided relief, but it felt horrible having it under my clothes all the time.

Even now, I still don't have a very good immune system. When it gets to winter and all the bugs start floating around I get chest infections and flu really easily. I take different supplements and vitamins to try and keep myself healthy, and always plenty of vitamin C and zinc. I also eat as healthily as possible. *Most* of the time.

I ate really well when I was growing up because my mum was so worried about my allergies she cooked everything from scratch, and if she gave me snacks it would always be fruit. I rarely had sweets and I didn't eat anything that was made in a factory or could have been contaminated in some way.

I was an only child for quite a while, and Mum says I'm the reason she waited so long to have another baby. I was pretty time-consuming and most of her energy went into getting and keeping me well. She actually wanted four kids, but I think I took up so much of her time she wondered how on earth she'd cope if she had that many.

I've got a stepbrother on my dad's side called Marvin, who is four years older than me. He used to come and stay with us at weekends from when I was a baby, and when he moved to London with his mum in his early teens he used to come and stay with us during the school holidays. That was the first time I ever experienced having a sibling and, luckily, we got on really well. We didn't have any of the usual brother-and-sister fights, probably because of the fact that we weren't with each other constantly.

My younger brother Kurtis came along when I was six. I remember being so excited. He was so tiny, and I couldn't wait for him to grow up so we could play together. I'd push him around in a pushchair like he was my little doll. As soon as he was old enough to walk I'd make him do kung fu with me. My mum would say I was pretty bossy with him, but I like to think it was character building.

He was a funny little boy and he was always getting up to mischief. One day when he was about three my mum left him in the living room for a matter of seconds, and when she walked back in he'd got hold of a big container of talcum powder and chucked it around. It was on the walls, the TV, the sofa – *everywhere*. How does a kid make such a big mess so quickly? My mum was horrified, but I was secretly impressed.

When he got a bit older we loved building forts together using bed sheets draped over sofas and chairs. I think my mum loved that *slightly* less than I did. We used to make such a mess but I think, on the plus side, it kept us quite quiet for hours on end.

We were close from the word go, and we still are now. We live together in Leeds when I'm in the UK, and it's like hanging out with a best mate rather than a brother. We like a lot of the same things and find each other's company really easy. Kurtis works as a football coach and an FA referee so, obviously, we both really like sport. He's a really hard worker and very bright, and he's graduated twice. The first time, he got a foundation degree with merit in sports coaching, and the second time he got a second-class honours degree 'second division' in sports studies, both from Leeds Metropolitan University.

Luckily, Kurtis didn't suffer health-wise in the same way I did. He was always a strong, healthy boy. These days, he's a strong, healthy man and people always think that he's my *older* brother because he's really tall and broad-shouldered whereas I'm quite petite. I always wanted to be taller growing up, but I'm too courageous as it is and I guess if I was taller I'd be even worse. That could have made me even more fearless.

I still get asked for ID all the time, despite being in my mid-thirties now. I even get asked when I go to a pharmacy to buy hayfever tablets, because you have to be over sixteen. My friends think it's hilarious, and I guess I should be grateful for it because most adults are trying to look younger. I don't do anything in particular, except stay healthy. I don't spend a fortune on crazy creams or anything. My mum still looks really young and she's got great skin so I've probably got her to thank. It's in the genes. Needless to say, the fact that I still look like a teenager is the reason I earned the nickname 'The Baby-faced Assassin', which is something I've been called for years. I honestly don't know who came up with it, it just kind of started.

Kurtis was the kid everyone wants, because he didn't cry and he was so easygoing. I reckon part of that was down to laziness – he didn't walk until he was two, whereas I was walking when I was six months. Apparently, I didn't even crawl in between.

I began walking one day when I was playing with a

pair of my booties and my mum took them away from me and put them on the sofa. She said I gave her this disapproving look and then dragged myself over to the sofa, pulled myself up and started walking along the side of it to get to the booties. My mum was shouting to my dad saying, 'Quick, Nikki's walking!' and he shouted back, 'Don't be ridiculous, she's only six months old! What are you talking about?' He couldn't believe it when he walked into the living room and I was standing there smiling at him. My mum says now that it must have been my steely determination making an early appearance.

Because I was walking at such a young age there was a possibility that I could have ended up becoming bow-legged because my bones still hadn't developed enough. They were too soft for me to stand on them and for a while it did look like my legs were starting to become the wrong shape. There was a chance I'd have to wear callipers, and I had to be monitored closely by a doctor. I was fine once my bones started to develop and get stronger and, thankfully, my legs straightened out. Clearly, once I learnt to walk, there was no stopping me.

My parents bought me one of those kiddie trolleys that's filled with wooden bricks so I could push myself along and, apparently, I loved it and was really independent. If they tried to help me do things, I'd get really cross because I wanted to do everything on my own.

I also loved nursery rhymes, and my mum used to

play me these educational ones, so I learnt all my times tables by the time I was four years old. When I started school my teacher was really impressed and asked my mum if she could take the tape into school so all the other kids could learn in the same way.

I spent my early years living on a council estate in East End Park, Leeds, which was as good as council estates get. It wasn't the roughest, but it was rough enough, and there wasn't much to do. The nice thing about the estate was that everyone looked out for each other. I spent most of the time chilling out with my friends. I guess it was more of an innocent time. The area wasn't always the best and we'd see the odd stolen car or motorbike zooming across the estate but, to be honest, that became a pretty normal sight after a while. I did have to be on my guard to a certain extent, but only in the way any kid does. A lot of my friends had older siblings so they often looked after us and made sure we were okay. I had really nice neighbours, and most of the kids in my street went to the same school as me. It was only three streets away so we'd all walk there and back together, so it did have a real community feel.

I loved school and I was really into science, so I thought maybe I'd go on to do something along those lines. At that point, becoming a boxer didn't even cross my mind. It was often on the TV in my house because my dad used to watch all the big fights and I enjoyed watching them with him, but I didn't ever think it was something I'd do myself.

I was good at maths at school and I was able to pick things up really quickly. English was never a big subject for me and I wasn't a big fan of reading and I'm still not. I was okay at art, but drama was much more my thing. I was in quite a few school plays. My first role was as a soldier in *The Nutcracker*. I was always very confident and I was a member of the choir so every Christmas we'd go to the local old people's home and perform for them. I haven't got the best voice in the world and I don't think *The X Factor* will be banging my door down any time soon, but I got by and I enjoyed it.

It won't come as much of a surprise that I liked sports when I was young and I was always running around the playground. My uncle Halstead – or Big H, as we called him – represented England at karate, and he used to teach me moves whenever he came to visit. I started doing classes at the local youth club and I got my yellow belt but I kind of lost interest. I don't know if karate is what gave me a taste for competitive sports, but I remember loving the feeling of strength and focus.

We were always playing competitive games as a family. We'd play Monopoly and Frustration. The latter was very appropriate, because we all wanted to win so much anyone who didn't would get so angry. I could never beat my dad at Connect 4 and when I was about six I said to him, 'Can't you just let me win one?' and he replied, 'No, because you won't appreciate the victory.' I've never forgotten that and, ever since then, I've worked tirelessly for what I want. I've never for a second expected anyone to hand me anything on a plate and because of that I appreciate every single bit of success I have.

I still play those games now and I still want to win everything.

I started playing chess when I was ten too, and I loved how tactical it was. You're always trying to make your opponent make a mistake and waiting for that moment where they have no choice but to submit. I played with my friends and Kurtis, and he went on to take part in competitions. He was better than me, which he still likes to remind me about.

Games are all about mental ability. Even Connect 4 taught me a lot. It's all about getting the edge over your opponent. They make moves they don't even realize they're making and when you see your opportunity you can swoop in and win.

I was never the kind of girl who played with dolls or liked dressing up. My mum was always trying to get me to wear pretty dresses but I hated them with a passion. She still dressed me up in awful frilly things if we went to a wedding or if I was having a school photo taken, but I wasn't happy about it. I'd have to be dragged out of the house, kicking and screaming, because I wanted to wear trousers or dungarees. Even now, I'm much more comfortable in trousers or suits, even if I have to go to a big event.

As I got a bit older, I liked watching films like *Star Wars* and the *Indiana Jones* movies, and I liked climbing trees in the park, playing football and bombing around on my BMX. We had a BMX park about ten minutes down the road that had loads of cool jumps, so I used to go there a lot. There was one jump called 'The Elephant's Back', and it was *so* steep. The first time I went on it I was so scared. I stood at the top for ages looking down, terrified I was going to hurt myself. Once I'd done it, though, I felt amazing and really confident, so I did it again and again. I think, because I was so active and always trying new things, I became pretty fearless. Then, one time, I got a bit over-confident and I fell off and busted my lip open. I was crying because I was wearing a new cream Nike tracksuit I'd been given for my birthday and I got blood all over it. I was more worried about what my mum was going to say about me ruining my tracksuit than about the pain.

I had a really mixed group of friends and I was mates with as many boys as I was girls. I had a few best friends, like Stacey, Kelly, Leon and Lyndon, and they were really similar to me and liked the same things, which was cool. We listened to a lot of music together. I was really into dance and R&B. I was never massively into pop bands, although I did go through a stage of liking NSYNC – but I don't like to talk about that now. It was just a blip. I wasn't a fan of S Club 7 or Steps. My mates and I thought we were too cool for all that. I loved Bob Marley too. My mum always use to play his music while she was in the kitchen cooking and even now when I hear his voice it transports me right back there and I can smell her Sunday roasts. My favourite track of his is 'Jammin'', and when I hear it I always feel really happy.

My early childhood was pretty mixed. Some of it was happy, like being able to hang out with my friends and have fun and going on holidays, and some of it was really tough, because my parents had a difficult relationship, to say the least. But some of my happiest memories are of going to New York for six weeks every year on holiday. We've got family over there so we'd go and visit them, and it was always something I looked forward to so much. We used to go to theme parks and my dad would take us to see things like the Statue of Liberty, the Empire State Building and the Twin Towers. It was so funny because we did the same things every year and sometimes I kind of wanted to say to my dad, 'You know the Statue of Liberty hasn't changed since last year, don't you? It's still a woman holding a torch? I just want to go to the water park.'

We used to go to a lot of theme parks in the UK as well, like Thorpe Park and Alton Towers. Mum and Dad always used to surprise us, so I'd only realize we were going once I saw the bags packed. I loved going on all of the rides. I used to get really frustrated because I wasn't tall enough for some of the big ones, and every year I used to go back hoping I'd have grown enough to be let on. Thankfully, Kurtis loved theme parks too so I've always had a partner in crime on that front, and we were both as fearless as each other.

Two:

Round One

After many years of rows and fights, my parents finally separated when I was eleven. I was so relieved. You see, their break-up wasn't exactly straightforward. It wasn't a case of two people not getting along any more. My mum had put up with a lot.

The first memory I have of their rows is from when I was three or four years old and my parents were fighting. I just wanted to get between them and stop it, so I jumped in front of my mum and tried to protect her with a plastic sword. I thought I could keep my dad away. My mum reckons that, even then, I was brave.

I was always aware that things weren't right between my parents, and their arguments became more frequent the older I got. I don't know if it's because I became more conscious of things, but I definitely felt like they were escalating.

I kept begging my mum to leave my dad and make a fresh start. I could never understand why she couldn't just walk away from him. To my young mind, it was so easy and straightforward. If things go badly, you up and leave. But now, of course, I know it's not that simple. I think it's incredibly hard to understand a situation like that unless you're in it yourself, especially because you're always hoping – and praying – that things will get better.

If you've got someone telling you they're going to change, you *want* to believe it. You remember how good things once were and hope it can get back to that. Plus, if you've got kids to think about, it must make it ten times as hard. It must have been so scary for my mum to think that she'd have two kids to raise on a single income.

My mum must have felt trapped. The alternative to that awful situation is having to change your life completely, and that can be just as terrifying as what you're already experiencing.

I don't know what switched for my mum but one day she snapped, and that was it – she'd had enough. From then on, things moved really quickly and within a matter of weeks we had moved out of our family home and were living in our new house. I'm so glad Kurtis was too young to remember any of the really awful times. I always did my best to protect him, and so did my mum.

I talked to Mum quite recently about how hard it must have been for her, and she says now that the reason she left in the end was because I kept asking her to. She also realized that, although she'd always thought she was protecting us by staying with my dad so we had financial security and a roof over our heads, that was never going to be enough.

I felt nothing but relief when Mum said she was

leaving my dad. I wasn't upset because I wouldn't see him, I just felt happy – and then very confused and guilty for feeling happy. I was relieved we weren't living with him any more but, at the end of the day, he was still my dad so of course I still missed him sometimes, despite everything.

I saw my dad every now and again after the break-up but I wasn't that bothered either way, if I'm being honest. He wasn't there for me growing up and he didn't offer me anything I didn't already have. I might get a present on my birthday or at Christmas sometimes but there was never any emotional support, which is a parent's most important job.

My mum pretty much brought me and Kurtis up on her own for the next few years. I know it was hard for her at times, but she didn't ever complain. She had two jobs following the divorce and she worked day and night. She was a governor at my first school, Richmond Hill Primary, for about six years, from when I was really young. She was a manager for a jewellery company and she also worked as a hairdresser. Later on, she became the manager of a restaurant. Sometimes she'd have to work until midnight and then get up early to go to her second job the next day.

She had a black uniform for one of her jobs and it had gone grey because she wore it so often and had to keep washing it. I can't fault her for how hard she worked to make sure my brother and I were looked after. She sacrificed a lot for us and she did everything she could to make sure we were okay.

She was working so hard and she was so busy raising us but she still found time to study communication skills, an alarm engineering course and a computer course. She also got a distinction in electronic servicing. She's always pushed herself so hard. I've never seen her out of work, and she always passed on to Kurtis and me how important education is.

We never wanted for love because my mum had more than enough for two parents and she supported us, no matter what. She was a great example of someone who knew they could do what they needed to if they put their mind to it. One year, she was in a terrible relationship, too scared to leave, and the next she was living in a new place and doing an amazing job of looking after two kids. We never, ever, felt like we missed out on things. Okay, we all had to make sacrifices sometimes and Mum probably couldn't buy the things she wanted, but she always found money for Kurtis and me when we needed it. I've always been determined that I will pay her back one day. I said to her when I was in my teens that there would come a day when she didn't ever have to struggle for anything again, and I meant it. That's been one of the main things that's driven me in my career.

I don't think what happened with my parents had a long-term effect on me emotionally, but I do think, if I didn't have such a strong character, it could easily have done. I felt angry a lot of the time growing up and I'm pretty sure you could link that back to the horrible things I witnessed when my parents were arguing. Thankfully, boxing gave me a way to channel it. I do wonder what things would have been like if I hadn't taken it up.

I was angry and confused. When I watched programmes on TV, it felt like the parents were always together. I didn't see many single parents, and I used to watch these happy families and think, *Why aren't mine like that?* No matter how hard parents try to make a separation easy on kids, it's always going to be difficult. The parents may still get on well, but it's going to have a knock-on effect, whatever happens.

There are ways of making things better, and we do still have choices. Luckily, I found boxing and I made the choice not to let the break-up affect my life long-term. I had a routine and I had something that empowered me and made me feel good. I could have chosen to go down a bad route but I wanted to do something good with my life and make my mum proud. I was determined that I was going to make my own life and that, no matter what it was I did, I was going to make myself into something great. I think that's one of the reasons my mum is so proud of me.

I had to become a grown-up from a young age and I guess, because my mum was working a lot, there were times when I acted like both a mum and a dad to Kurtis.

I always told my mum that one day we could be a happy family and we'd be able to buy what we wanted. The first bit is certainly true and I'm working on the second. I do feel like I've got the happy family I always wanted now. My mum's life, and Kurtis's and mine, haven't been totally plain sailing and there have been rough times to get through but it's been so worth it.

After my parents split up, my mum, Kurtis and I moved to another housing estate. Everybody who lived there was given a house for a reason, and that reason was to help them to move on from a bad situation, whatever that may be.

I would say that was the first time I experienced real fear, because all of a sudden my world was turned upside down. I'd gone from living with both my parents in an area I knew really well and liked to living somewhere totally new where I didn't know anyone. I spent quite a lot of time on my own in the early days because, although I saw my mates at school, at the end of the day they'd all troop off home together to our old estate. There were times when I felt pretty lonely and I missed everyone but I knew we'd moved for the right reasons so I had to keep reminding myself of that whenever I felt sad.

I felt a bit all over the place at first, and I found myself having to make new friends. But, on the plus side, I got my own room, so I didn't have to share with Kurtis any more, which was a massive bonus. I didn't mind sharing with my brother, because we had quite a laugh most of the time, but I did torment him quite a bit so I think he was probably relieved to have his own space.

I had a catapult that I used to take everywhere with me and one time when I was about seven I was on the top level of our bunk and I bent down and fired a Lego brick and it hit him in the middle of his head. He put his hand straight to his head and I was wetting myself, but then he burst into tears and, when he took his hand away, I saw that he had a small cut and I started panicking. He started screaming and I kept saying, 'Shush! Shush!' because I knew that if my parents found out what I'd done they would go mad. My dad shouted up the stairs, asking what was going on, and Kurtis replied, 'Nicola's just shot me in the head!' I got into so much trouble and my catapult got confiscated. It joined the box of other toys I'd had taken away from me, including a bow and arrow I used to use to shoot at Mum's ornaments.

My mum and dad kept my repossessed toys on top of a high cupboard in the kitchen so I couldn't get to them but, being a strong-willed little girl, I wasn't going to let a little thing like that stand in my way. I worked out that if I opened the bottom cupboard door I could stand on it, climb up on to the work surface and just about reach them. It was like a mini assault course but it was so worth it. I'd always have to remember to put them back before anyone noticed but it meant I got to enjoy them for a little while.

I was pretty fearless at that age and I used to sit at the top of this big conker tree near my house, really still, so no one knew I was there, and I'd throw conkers at people as they walked past.

Even though I could be a bit mischievous, I wasn't the kind of kid to get into fights, as you might think. And certainly not in secondary school, because I was already boxing by then. I probably wasn't the right person to pick on. There was one boy who used to pick on everyone at my primary school. He was in the year above me and one day I'd had enough and threw my little toy truck at him. I got into real trouble with the teachers, and I was scared as hell when I went to school the following day because I thought he would want to get his revenge on me but, actually, after that, he left everyone alone and he was really nice to me. I think that happens a lot. Once you stand up to bullies, they tend to back down. I learnt a really good lesson that day. Often, bullies are the ones who are the most insecure, and as soon as someone puts them in their place they lose their power.

There wasn't a lot I was afraid of as a kid, but I hated spiders and I still do now. I was always scared of ghosts too, because I used to watch a lot of horror movies but, thankfully, I grew out of that. I've learnt that ghosts aren't real. Sadly, spiders are.

It took me a good few months to settle into our new house and I was over the moon when I looked out of my bedroom window one day and spotted three friends who I'd been to nursery school with. It turned out they'd moved on to the estate as well, because their parents had been dealing with various issues. Things started looking up after that, because I had familiar faces around me and I had people to talk to who were going through similar things. We had different issues and problems but we came together and supported each other.

My school was quite near our new house, but Kurtis's was twenty minutes away and I used to have to walk him there and back each day because my mum was working. When he eventually moved to the school at the end of my street, it made things much easier. My mum describes us as 'latchkey kids' because we had to look after ourselves a lot at quite an early age, but I didn't mind it at all. I was just happy that my mum was happy. I noticed such a massive difference in her after she left my dad and I was so proud that she'd finally had the courage to start a new life.

In a way, my new life started not long after we moved, because that's when I discovered boxing. My mum was due to go to an aerobics class at Burmantofts Boxing Club and the babysitter cancelled at the last minute. She couldn't find anyone else, so she had to take Kurtis and me along with her. We were too young to be trusted to stay in on our own.

She went in to do her aerobics and Kurtis and I waited in the gym outside, which happened to be a boxing gym. I remember looking around and seeing everyone doing boxing training. I was so taken aback. It was like nothing I'd ever seen before. The super heavyweights were pounding away on bags, and people were sparring each other. It was like a proper, old-school, *Rocky*-style gym, with steamed-up windows and peeling paint. I instantly fell in love with the place. I stood there and thought, *This must have been what it was like for Muhammad Ali when he was starting out.*

Ali had always been a big idol of mine, because I used to watch all of his fights on TV with my dad. But even though I found boxing fascinating and I was always really sporty at school, I hadn't imagined for a minute it was something I might do one day.

That evening, I had a choice of either sitting around or getting involved in the boxing. The coach, Steve Franks, asked if I fancied giving it a go, and I thought, *Why not?* The first thing the coach got me to do was pads, and I can't explain why but it just felt *right* and I wanted to do more. When I got home that night I couldn't stop talking about it and I begged my mum to take me back.

The gym ran a junior boxing club and an after-school club, so that were perfect for me. The more I went, the more hooked I got (no pun intended). Something about it got to me, and I felt like the people there got *me*.

Over the next couple of weeks I learnt to shadow box and I soon perfected my stance and started learning to jab. I didn't think about the fact that it was such a male environment and I was this young girl. I loved being there so much. Steve said really early on that the gym wasn't male or female, it was just a boxing gym. He had one rule and that was that we all listened to him. Aside from that, it was pretty laid back.

Steve always made me feel like I was no different from anyone else there, and one day he took my mum aside and told her he thought I had real potential. Even though my mum was already fine with me boxing, I think that's what made her realize that it could turn into more than just a hobby for me.

When I turned thirteen, Mum started letting me go to the gym on my own and Steve would drop me home afterwards. I had to spar with guys a lot and quite often I gave them a good run for their money. My brother started boxing a bit as well and I used to spar with him sometimes, which I loved. He was only about eight years old but he always thought he could beat me – but there was no way!

None of my female friends boxed, but a couple of my guy mates from secondary school did, so I knew people at the gym already, and I soon made more friends. I didn't see it as a big deal, and none of my mates, male or female, did either. Maybe if I'd started later it would have seemed strange, but twelve is an age where you're discovering what you like. You don't analyse things or create problems or reasons you shouldn't do something. You follow your heart and you don't think of the consequences.

It was Muhammad Ali and my mum that inspired me most when I was younger. Ali was such a character and I loved his rhymes. I picked up different moves from watching his fights and I still do now. I still watch him on YouTube all the time and he never fails to give me focus.

My mum is amazing for all the reasons you'll read about in this book, and she's also my number-one superfan. When people ask her, 'How did you know you were raising a champion?' she always replies, 'I didn't know I was!' She pretends she takes it all in her stride but I know she's so proud of everything Kurtis and I have achieved. She was always positive about everything I did and she told me I could be as good as Muhammad Ali. If there are any words a young, aspiring boxer needs to hear, it's those ones.

I used to go to the gym three times a week while my friends were going out together, so I did miss out on cinema trips or hanging out in the park every now and again, but I really didn't mind. It wasn't like anyone was forcing me to go to the gym and sometimes it was more enjoyable for me than doing anything else.

I'd been training for a year when Steve asked me if I was interested in going into competitions. It was the obvious next step and I was really excited about the prospect. Even though some of my friends thought it was a pretty big deal, I didn't feel nervous at all. It felt like the right time and I was ready to box in front of a crowd.

My first match took place in a working men's club in Leeds when I was thirteen. My family came along to watch me and I was so excited I kept peeping through the curtains to look at the audience. Steve kept telling me off because he wanted me to conserve my energy for the match, but I was totally buzzing. I don't think you have a lot of fear at that age, do you? I just wanted to get out into the ring and show people what I could do. I was allowed to pick my own song to walk out to and I chose Ini Kamoze's 'Here Comes the Hotstepper'.

I'd been watching a lot of Prince Naseem's fights, so when I stepped into the ring I started doing his moves, like the shuffle, and engaging with the audience. Putting on a show has been really important to me since day one, because boxing should be about entertainment as much as everything else. I like knowing that the crowd are enjoying themselves. I wasn't scared about getting hit because I'd been boxing for a year and I knew that, if it did happen, I'd take it all in my stride.

I think that was the first time most of the people in the club had seen a girl box, and I imagined they would all carry on drinking their pints and chatting to each other but, amazingly, they all paid attention. I was pleasantly surprised. The only downside was that the match took place before the smoking ban came in and the entire room was thick with smoke, which really hurt the back of my throat. I was pretty out of breath at times. I can't imagine being able to do a full-on tournament now if people still smoked. It's the last thing my asthma needs.

I remember going back to the corner at the end of the first and second rounds. My lungs were on fire. Steve told me stories about how, when he boxed as a youngster, even the coach was allowed to smoke. He'd be trying to get his breath back in the middle of a match and his coach would be blowing smoke in his face. Can you imagine? The smoking ban is one of the best things that has ever happened, in my opinion.

I won the match and, straight away, I was determined to keep going and win more. I'd found something that I not only loved but that I was really good at. That was the moment I decided that, one day, I was going to be the best and I was also going to be an Olympic champion. When I look back now, it was a pretty unrealistic dream because women's boxing wasn't an Olympic sport and showed no sign of being one in the near future. But I was *so* sure. I just had this 'knowing'. When I used to tell people I was going to win Olympic gold they'd laugh at me, but I didn't care. One day, I was going to prove them all wrong.

Aside from spending a lot of time in the gym, I was like any other normal kid. I was really into the TV show *Gladiators*, and when they brought out a kids' version I was desperate to be on it. I went to the cinema with my mates a lot and I watched films like *Jumanji*, *Honey, I Shrunk the Kids* and *Tomb Raider* at home with my brother. I loved anything that had a bit of adventure in it.

A lot of my friends were going down to the park and drinking in their early teens and, although I used to go and hang out with them sometimes, I couldn't drink because of training. It would have been a nightmare trying to punch bags with a hangover. If I ever did a run on a hangover, I could feel the alcohol coming out of my pores and it really affected my stamina.

I still got to chill out with my mates and I used to go to this nightclub for kids every month. I went there religiously from about the age of fourteen to sixteen, and it was good because it was somewhere we could go and dance before we were allowed to go to grown-up places. It was like an in-between kind of place. I was lucky that, even though I was really dedicated to my training, I did get to do other things outside of it. I had a good balance growing up and boxing didn't get really competitive until I was older, so I still had a lot of freedom, which was important to me.

I think having a balance has always been important. For instance, I enjoy a drink, but I'm not someone who goes out and gets really drunk. I enjoy myself if I'm on a night out but, obviously, if I've got a big tournament coming up I'll abstain for a while beforehand while I'm getting myself into the best condition I can. I'll be honest, it's not unusual for athletes to let themselves go sometimes.

Everyone wants to enjoy themselves, but it's about choosing the right times to do it.

My mum was always really supportive of my boxing and she was pleased I was doing something that I enjoyed and which kept me busy. She didn't ever worry about me getting hurt either. She knew my mind-set, so she knew I'd do everything to ensure that didn't ever happen. I always told her the name of the game is to hit but not get hit back.

I've never been injured by someone else as a result of boxing and I've never been knocked out. The first time I got a punch that hurt me I got caught right on the end of my nose and it made my eyes water. It was a bit of a shock, and I remember thinking *Ow!*, but then I just carried on. It didn't affect me at all because I'd been training for so long and there were some times when I was sparring that someone would catch me at the wrong angle. At the end of the day, if you step in a shower you're going to get wet, and if you're in a boxing ring you know you might get hit, so it's not like I didn't expect it to happen.

My mum is very strong-willed as well, and I probably got a lot of my determination from her. I grew up admiring how she dealt with everything and how, even when things were tough, she picked herself up and carried on. She made me believe that you could do it all. She was strong, but she was also feminine. She handled everything that came her way but she still managed to be caring and kind, and it was rare to catch her without make-up on and her hair done. She took a lot of pride in her appearance and in herself as a person, and that radiated from her.

Kurtis continued boxing for a while but he wasn't keen on how much time the training took up. He enjoyed the boxing but he could take or leave the rest of it, so he didn't stick at it for very long. I loved the tough training, and I still do. Most of all, I loved the way the more you put into training, the more you got out of it. It was a simple equation: the better you were at training, the better boxer you would become.

A typical training session for me in those early days would involve a run, work on the training pads and punch bag, sparring and a circuit. It wasn't like the GB training camps I went to later on, where you separated everything out and had time off in between. I did everything in one session, and it's still like that in a lot of clubs. Generally, I would end up doing a three-hour session with barely a break. I don't know how I was able to do it. I couldn't do it now. I guess my body got used to it, but I couldn't go back to doing such an intense session with no proper breaks.

For some reason, when it came to sports, I was always better competing on my own. I played rounders and basketball at school, but I wasn't keen on basketball because, one time, the ball hit my finger and I couldn't bend it for days. I know it sounds ridiculous that I was worried about that when I was boxing big, burly guys, but I found that more painful than taking a knock.

I liked playing some team sports, but I didn't like the fact that I'd be working really, really hard and then I'd lose because someone else in the team wasn't working as hard as me. It used to really frustrate me. I think I always knew I would be better in an individual sport where there weren't people that let the side down. Harsh, but true.

The other kids liked having me on their team because I was a good all-rounder, but they weren't that keen on competing against me. I always had the edge in any sport and I was the fastest in the school. On sports day, I used to come home with so many trophies. The teachers would make me take part in every race and event going, and every year the other kids were probably hoping I'd get ill and miss it. I was a good runner and ran for Leeds City when I was fourteen. I took part in a few competitions but in the end I decided that I wanted to concentrate on boxing as much as possible, and I didn't have time to do both.

Secondary school was a pretty good time for me, and the things I enjoyed doing most were music classes and playing the drums. I was never in a band or anything but I did learn some of the drum beats and I loved the feeling of thrashing around. I guess it was another way to channel my excess energy.

I was a bit of a joker so I did get in trouble at times, but I wasn't purposely disruptive. I was diagnosed with ADHD when I was thirteen so I found it hard to stay still in big groups of classes and I liked messing around with my classmates more than listening to what the teacher was saying. I couldn't concentrate very well and every little thing used to distract me.

Having ADHD definitely affected me, because I used to get frustrated at not being able to pick things up as easily as some of the other pupils could. The only subjects I could really pay attention in were science and maths, and that's because they interested me, but everything else used to go over my head. I did try, I really did, but I didn't find things like English easy at all. I couldn't get to grips with the books we'd be made to read. I'm still the same now. I do like books but I find it hard to concentrate, so I prefer listening to audio books while I'm driving. I find them so much easier to understand. I wish I'd been allowed to listen to audio books when I was at school, to be honest. I probably would have done a lot better in my English exam.

Luckily, I was a pretty strong character so I didn't allow having ADHD to knock my confidence. I tried taking medication for a while, but I didn't like the tablets because they made me feel spaced out. Looking back, I should maybe have tried some others to see if they were any better, because they might have been really helpful, but I was worried about them having an adverse effect on me.

Of course, boxing was a brilliant outlet for ADHD. It was always my 'go to' thing if I was ever feeling overwhelmed, and I suppose I used it as a form of medication.

As I got into my mid-teens there was pressure to decide what I wanted to do career-wise, but I already knew. Obviously, I was going to be a champion boxer. My teachers weren't always that receptive when I told them my plans. I remember so clearly one of them saying to me, 'That's a lovely idea, but women's boxing isn't even in the Olympics.' I replied, 'Yeah, but one day it will be, and I'll be taking home gold.' I wouldn't let anyone put me off.

Three:

My Mum's Big Fight

When I was fourteen something happened that shaped me more than anything else in my life has ever done. My mum nearly died. It was one of the scariest times of my life and, even though it was over twenty years ago now, when I think back to it, it still makes me feel completely breathless.

I remember getting ready to go out one Saturday and my mum telling me she was feeling really unwell. She had flu symptoms and, as the day went on, they got worse and worse. My mum's friend took her to see an out-of-hours doctor, and by that point she was in such a bad way the doctor offered to examine her in the waiting room because she was so weak. In the end, he had to help her walk from the waiting area into his office. He gave Mum a thorough examination and told her it was likely she had some kind of flu or infection so he sent her home with some co-codamol and told her to get some rest.

When I got back home that evening she looked so ill I panicked. She was finding it hard to walk and her speech seemed a bit slurred, but she insisted she would be fine. She was sweating, so I got her undressed and gave her a bath, hoping that would help, but all she wanted to do was sleep. When I eventually got her into bed she couldn't move and she looked like she was slipping in and out of consciousness. I thought she was probably exhausted or maybe having a bad reaction to her medication. I tried talking to her but she wasn't responding properly, and when she did she wasn't making much sense. I started to get really worried so I called an ambulance, but it seemed to take forever to arrive. I was phoning them constantly and begging them to hurry up. When they finally arrived, they took one look at her and said they had to get her to hospital as soon as possible because they thought she'd had a stroke.

She was rushed to St James's Hospital, where she was put in a bed in a ward. She was being monitored, but she was left for three hours before I put my foot down and demanded something was done. I was genuinely scared she was going to die. Kurtis was with me and he was only young, so I was trying to stay calm for him, but I was so angry that she was being ignored. At last, they started to pay proper attention to her, and I was so grateful. I do understand that hospitals get very busy and that they do an incredible job of taking care of people, but I hate to think what would have happened if Mum had been left without help for any longer. By that point, she couldn't even remember her own date of birth or how many children she had. When they asked her how many kids she had she said that she had two daughters, she was so confused.

They did loads of tests, including a lumbar puncture, which is supposed to be one of the most painful proced-ures you can have. Poor Mum was so out of it she didn't feel a thing. Her body had started to shut down and go into shock so she was numb all over.

When the doctors got the test results back, they diag-nosed meningitis and said her brain had already started to shut down. If she hadn't gone to hospital when she did, the likelihood is she would have died. She only had a couple of hours to live when they started giving her the right treatment.

Mum doesn't remember a thing about her first few days in hospital. When she eventually woke up she had hearing loss in her right ear, which they think may have been caused by both the illness and the medication she was given to treat it. She's now completely deaf in her right ear and she still suffers from tinnitus in both ears. On a bad day, she has real trouble hearing, which she finds frustrating.

It was really tough while she was in hospital because, not only was I worried about Mum, I also had to stay strong for my brother. He was only eight years old at the time and I didn't want him to see me upset and then become worried. I wanted him to think everything was okay. He needed someone to tell him that, without ques-tion, our mum was going to pull through.

I kept everything bottled up for as long as possible and then, one day, I was sat in the hospital canteen and everything got on top of me. I suddenly felt so over-whelmed by everything that had happened. I burst into tears. I think the seriousness of the situation had finally hit me and, once I started crying, I couldn't stop. Thankfully, the canteen was pretty empty. I would have been mortified if I'd been crying my eyes out in front of a load of total strangers, but I think it was something I really needed to do.

Mum had to stay in hospital for a month. It was such a relief when she finally came back home, but she still had a long way to go to recover. She couldn't balance properly because of her hearing loss, so she had to learn how to get around again using a walking stick. I had to do the washing, make dinner and keep the house clean because, as much as she wanted to help out (remember how determined I said she was?), she just didn't have the energy.

I had to get Kurtis up and ready in the morning, make him breakfast and then take him to school and pick him up. Most of Mum's family live down south in Ipswich and her mum lives in Nottingham, so it wasn't like they were really close by, so they couldn't come and help. It was just the three of us, really. The Three Musketeers, like it pretty much always has been. I do think Mum's illness made me realize just how much she had been doing for me and Kurtis up until that point, and how amazing she was to juggle all the different things she had going on. My mum means the absolute world to me, but that was when I started really appreciating how amazing she was.

My friends and their parents were really considerate and helpful and always said I could go to them if I needed anything but, really, we were on our own a lot of the time. Mum was desperate to get well so she could start looking after us again, but it was a slow process and not one that could be rushed. She was ill, and she was so achey and tired she said that she constantly felt like she was trying to walk through treacle.

The only time Mum went out during that time was when Kurtis and I took her down to the supermarket. We'd wheel the trolley around and she'd tell us what groceries to put in it.

Mum being so unwell was an awful experience but it definitely made me stronger, and it made me love my family more than ever. You always think that kind of thing will happen to someone else. It feels very unbelievable that it happened to Mum. I also feel like, whatever I go through in the future, it can never be as bad as that. I can handle anything that comes my way because nothing will ever feel as terrible as Mum being ill did.

The doctors said it would take about five years for my mum to fully recover and, even now, she's not 100 per cent. She's learnt how to walk again and, although she'll never be 'normal', it's amazing that she's got to the point she has. Her sight is slightly worse than it was, but you would never know because she still does everything she always did. Her hearing will never be the same, and she used to shout a lot because of her hearing loss but now she talks at the same volume as everyone else.

She gets aches in her shoulders and she has days when she's in quite a lot of pain generally, but she's not one to moan about it. If she wants help, she'll ask for it, but she's very stoic and she gets on with things as well as she can. She knows that my brother and I are always there if she needs us.

I think the fact that I had to stay positive throughout that experience taught me new skills. I've never been the type of person to panic and imagine the worst but, since then, I've taken everything in my stride. To a certain extent, you have a choice how you react to things, and I know there's no point in getting stressed, because it doesn't change anything. By remaining calm, I usually find ways to get the best outcome, and there is generally a solution to every problem.

Of course, I still come up against obstacles in life sometimes, because who doesn't? But as long as I've got my family, that's the most important thing to me, and nothing can ever be as big a deal as Mum's illness was. It made me re-evaluate how I thought about everything.

Obviously, what happened to Mum shook her up a lot. I think it gave her a 'life's too short' attitude. She had been single since separating from my dad and when she started to get better she began dating a little bit, and that's when she met her good friend Ray. Luckily, Kurtis and I got on with him straight away and he's a really good guy. It can be tricky when a parent meets someone else after a divorce, but he wasn't fazed that my mum had kids and he made a real effort to get to know us.

Ray and my mum aren't an item, and they're not married or anything like that, but I look on him as a stepdad. He's always been there for us. My mum has such a good heart and people have taken advantage of her in the past, but Ray is a really nice guy and they get on so well.

He's always been really chilled out and supportive of my boxing, unlike my real dad, who told me I should forget about boxing, college and university and go and get a real job. My late grandfather, Franklin Ottley, always believed that education was the key to life. He passed that belief down to my mum, who, thankfully, passed it on to Kurtis and me, so I always wanted to study.

After slowing down my training a bit when Mum was ill, I started going back to the gym regularly, and I was really ready for another fight. I was always hassling Steve to set up another match, but there were no junior women for me to box so I had to wait another five years to get into the ring competitively again. It was very frustrating at times and Steve was constantly looking around for other girls for me to fight, but there just weren't any.

Back in the early days, it was down to my coaches to try and find out about tournaments I could get involved in. Because women's boxing was still such a small thing, there wasn't any kind of network in place. It was a case of Steve calling around other gyms to set up some sparring or a match. Then, of course, there was the cost involved in travelling so, all in all, it wasn't terribly easy.

I'd still box with the lads at the gym sometimes, but it just wasn't the same as being in the ring fighting competitively. I'd watch all the guys excitedly going off to different competitions and I'd have to plod along and keep sparring. There were times when I got so sick of it I wondered if I was doing the right thing dedicating so much to something when I wasn't getting the opportunities I wanted. But yet, I knew, one day, things would change.

I had this sense that it would all be okay. I don't know where it came from but I've always had good intuition so I put it down to that. Intuition can be an amazing driving force, but people don't always listen to it. Sometimes we've got so many different people's voices in our ears telling us what we should do it's hard to listen to our own voice, so when the noise from other people got too loud I would take a step back and remember that things had always worked out when I'd trusted myself.

My coach, Steve, was always there by my side, supporting me. He also worked as a taxi driver and it was funny because, as I got older and started going on nights out, he'd sometimes end up taking me home. He'd say to me, 'Remember you've got to do a run in the morning!' Sometimes when he got off a shift at 6 a.m. he'd come and sit outside my house to make sure I was up and out on time. Other times he'd knock on the door at ridiculous times and offer to run with me because he was worried I wouldn't get out of bed and train if it was wet and cold.

He taught me a lot early on, and I think the main things I took away from working with him was to be confident in myself and not to let anyone stop me following my dreams. He was always telling me how good I was and that one day everyone would see it. That, coupled with my own self-confidence, was a winning formula.

Some people said I was crazy and that I would never make it all the way to the Olympics, but I didn't let them bring me down. I didn't ever falter and there was never a time when I doubted I would go on to be really successful. I didn't have a plan B as back-up if I wasn't. For me, it was boxing or nothing.

I did become a bit despondent for a while and wondered if I'd ever have the opportunity to fight again, and it wasn't until I was seventeen and turned senior that I got the chance to box someone else.

I was so excited about finally having another competition to take part in. My mum, my brother, my uncle Robert and Steve Franks came to London with me. It was a day I'll never forget. I designed my own boxing kit and had it made; it was black, white and silver with tassels. It had 'Adams' written on the back and 'Babyface' down the side. I won that fight as a result of a knockout in the second round, and after that I had a few more fights here and there and felt like the pace was finally picking up.

By then I was also working with another brilliant coach called Fred Gummerson at the Hard and Fast AMC Boxing Club in Barnsley. It was a great place and they always looked after me. Fred set up more tournaments for me, and one of the first big ones I went to was Yorkshire versus Canada. The club funded me, so they paid for my travel out to Canada, as well as my food. All their money was raised via sponsors and they would help out all the kids who belonged to their club as often as they could.

I was travelling up and down to London a lot, training in various different gyms and clubs, and throughout it all Fred and Steve were there for me. Sometimes I'd have to get the train back to Leeds pretty late and Steve would come and pick me up from the train station and take me home so he knew I was safe. I was so grateful for all he did for me.

The Amateur Boxing Association of England (ABAE) had given the go-ahead for women to box in 1996, when I was fourteen. I went to a sports hall in Crystal Palace for trials to try to get a place in the England squad, alongside all of the other female boxers in the country. We were put through a number of assessments, so we had to do bleep tests, where we had to run back and forth between two points 20 metres apart in time with 'bleeps' to assess our fitness levels, and spar so the coaches could see how technically skilled we were. At that point, there was, effectively, no women's team, and there never had been, so no one really knew what to do with us.

Obviously, there was a massive element of competition so, while everyone was friendly to each other, we all knew we were rivals. We were all concentrating on what we needed to do, and in my case that was winning the upcoming National Championships in Hendon, London.

I wore my silver, black and white kit again when I competed, and my coach, Steve, was with me. Because I didn't have many people on my side at that time, it was so important to have a few people who totally believed in me. He always totally trusted that I was going to make it, and if ever I doubted myself he'd be the first one to tell me not to.

I won the National Championships fighting a girl called Leah, and it was very cool to be able to say that I was national champion and therefore the best in England. As a result of that I got a place in the newly formed national squad. That was the best moment of my life up until then, and I was so happy.

After I won the National Championships, I had my first international fight, in Dublin, Ireland, in a tournament called Boxing Ireland. It was the first time I got the chance to spend proper time with other female boxers. They picked two girls out of the entire line-up of UK women's boxers, and one of them was me. This involved me flying over to Dublin and boxing a number of other girls. I flew over on the Friday, boxed on the Saturday in a one-off fight and flew back on the Sunday.

Even though I won my match in Dublin, nothing changed in terms of the women's team. The organization was terrible and there was no structure in place for us. It was like we were seen as some kind of joke – like a novelty act you get on *Britain's Got Talent* who are quite entertaining but you don't want to invest too much energy in.

The ABAE had basically been forced into letting females have some of the same opportunities as men because we'd hassled them so much. We tried to get women's boxing talked about in the media more, to raise awareness. But their attitudes certainly didn't change overnight. We were still left to fend for ourselves.

The boys' national team got to go to training camps at the English Institute of Sport in Crystal Palace really regularly, and they also had the opportunity to train there whenever they wanted to. Women, however, were only allowed if they were invited, so we'd have to wait for an organized training camp, which were rare, to be able to use the facilities.

Despite the fact that we were training for the same competitions, we weren't a priority; the men came first and we had no choice but to take a back seat. I knew it was backwards at the time but, looking back now, it seems even more shocking. A lot of the girls had great ability, but no one had any faith in us. How were we supposed to get better if we didn't have the *means* to get better? We believed in ourselves but it felt like none of the other people we needed to believe in us did. I kind of get it, because people are often afraid of things that are new and have never been done before.

The stupid thing is that none of the male boxers was in any way bothered about the fact that we were women and they were always really friendly and encouraging towards us. It was the coaches who had an issue with it; they saw boxing as a male sport. It's like people saying men shouldn't do synchronized swimming or gymnastics. Why on earth not? Who makes the rules on what men and women *should* do? Those kinds of attitudes are so old fashioned.

We women boxers were left to our own devices to carry on training at our own clubs at various places around the country, and we still didn't have a clue when or where any tournaments were taking place. We'd get a letter out of the blue, saying, 'There's a tournament next weekend and you've been selected. You have to go to a training camp and then you're going to Norway.' The organizers would have known about it for months but, for us, it was always so last minute it was ridiculous. How could we be expected to be ready for a tournament with so little warning or training? It felt like they didn't take us seriously.

It was frustrating, and it constantly felt like the coaches

were giving us something then taking it away again. On the one hand, they said they believed in us but, on the other, they didn't want to invest any time or money in us. If we didn't win medals, that would make them even more reluctant to make women boxers any kind of priority. But how could they expect us to win medals when they made so little effort and we were so under-prepared? It was a real chicken-and-egg situation, and it felt like they were always hedging their bets *just* in case we did start to become real contenders. We still had to do a lot of self-funding, which meant my mum was paying for a lot of my training. My club also helped out when they could, which was amazing of them.

In total contrast to the UK, Ireland had a really good training set-up, so I used to spend a lot of time over there, training with Katie Taylor, who I became really good friends with. I was so determined to succeed I was willing to travel anywhere to have access to good facilities. In the UK, we didn't have access to a single physio, so if we did get injured we'd have to use the physios from Ireland, and that was only if we were taking part in a tournament.

They were so much more advanced than us. When Katie started winning medals her dad went to the Irish Amateur Boxing Association and asked for funding and, because they could see how much potential she had, they gave it to her. But even though I was winning medals, I got nothing. My mum was doing her best, and she wrote to all kinds of people and made phone calls on my behalf to try and get sponsorship and funding. She contacted the ABAE so many times, but all they kept telling her was, 'It's not an Olympic sport,' so she got nowhere. She also applied to Leeds council for a sports grant and even wrote to local MPs. She got some really nice replies but, sadly, no offers to help me out.

It was pretty dangerous not having a physio, because one of the problems with any sport is that you don't always know when you've been injured. As I'll talk about in more detail later, I fractured one of my knuckles in my right hand when I was boxing in the quarter-finals of the European Championships in 2007 and then boxed twice more and won silver, not realizing that I was injured. It was the Irish physio who had to step in and help me. Luckily, my brother is an in-house first aider so he was able to help me at times too.

The old England coach, Mick Gannon, wasn't the nicest person either. It wasn't that he was against women's boxing as such, but he wasn't very supportive. I got out of the ring following one match which I'd lost due to an injury and he told me to go and watch a video of the bout and see how bad I was. It wasn't the most motivational speech I've ever had.

It makes such a big difference if people in positions of power help those who are trying to get to where they want to be. Equally, it can be very damaging if they do the opposite.

Luckily, Mick no longer has a job in the boxing set-up, which is a very good thing, because I would hate it if he was discouraging other girls. There's just no need for that. The women's team became an outlet for his unhappiness, but he was a nightmare. If you didn't agree with everything he said, you risked a dressing down. He didn't like other people's views. There were times when I wanted to have my say, but I didn't dare, not because I was scared of upsetting him, but because, at that time, he had a lot of say.

Sadly, it's pretty obvious that there was a really big element of sexism involved in the world of boxing. It was something I came up against a lot. It sounds like something out of the dark ages, but we were treated like second-class citizens, which is crazy in this day and age. Things have moved on so much, but it's only because women have proved themselves in such a big way. The England women's football team are amazing and, of course, the women's hockey team won an Olympic gold in Rio. But it's only because of achievements like this that people are sitting up and taking notice. It's a shame people can't have some faith before someone is holding a medal in their hands.

There's still a long way to go, but women's sport definitely gets more coverage than it did, and at least it's all a step in the right direction. Paula Radcliffe became so famous because she was the first woman to do long-distance running, bearing in mind that, back in the day, women weren't allowed to run very far because men thought our insides would fall out. *Seriously*.

The reason women weren't allowed to box before 1996 is because, apparently, our menstrual cycles make us unstable. I wish I was joking. It's like they thought a woman was going to go into the ring with PMT and lose control. That isn't even that long ago, which is the scary thing. But then I guess it wasn't that long ago that women couldn't vote either.

Jane Couch was a pioneer of women's boxing and she won a landmark court case in the late nineties to enable women to box. I was quite young when it all happened but I was always aware that she'd done it. She really got the ball rolling for women in the UK. Even once she won that case, there was still such a narrow-minded attitude, and it was suggested that women should have to wear skirts in the ring. Can you imagine? I mean, you're playing an active sport, not going on a date. If you want to, you should have the choice, so it should be optional, but you can't force someone to box in something that's clearly unsuitable.

I basically did anything I could to get ahead when I was trying to get women's boxing noticed, so I also went to Denmark and France to train several times. When tournaments were taking place (which wasn't nearly often enough) coaches would sometimes invite boxers from other countries to go over and spar so everyone could get warmed up. Every country has a different fighting style so it gave me some great experience, and it's something I still do to this day.

Sometimes when you're abroad you get to stay in really nice hotels, and other times you're in a dorm. You never really know what you're getting until you arrive. Nice food is always a massive draw for me, and it's often the main thing I'll remember about a place. I can easily name the places that have the best food. The US camp in Colorado has the best canteen of all the training camps. They have every soft drink you can think of, and McDonald's ice cream on tap. That's a real highlight for me. I don't go too crazy when I'm training, but I am allowed treats. I'll never forget the Sunday roasts at The Lodge, which is the accommodation for the English Institute of Sport at Crystal Palace. It was unbelievable and I still miss it to this day.

It was incredibly infuriating because, on occasion, I would be desperate to go to certain training camps, but I just couldn't afford it. My coaches and I tried to get our own funding but we hit so many brick walls. All me and the other female boxers wanted was for someone to give us a bit of a boost and help us on to the first rung of the ladder. We were happy to take it from there, but we needed that lift up first.

I'd look around at the male boxers, and it felt like they had everything. They had gyms and their kits paid for, and we were scrabbling around for the smallest crumbs. It was so bad that, even when we went away to fight for

England, we'd often be given kits that didn't fit properly. We'd have to take whatever was on offer and give them back afterwards.

Quite often, there wasn't enough kit to go round so we'd have to share. One girl would finish boxing and immediately hand her top and shorts to whoever was boxing next. It would be dripping in sweat and you'd have to dry everything out so you could wear it for your bout. Sometimes there wasn't enough time to dry it so you'd have to go into the ring in a wet kit someone else had just worn.

I was really lucky that, when I was in my early twenties, the tourism agency Welcome to Yorkshire started helping me out, and Hilton, the hotel company, also stepped in and started sponsoring my kit, so that was one less thing to worry about. My mum used to go to the gym at the Hilton hotel in Leeds and one day she told the manager about me. They told her they'd fund a kit for me and I could go in and use the gym for free. I also got discounted rates on hotels when I travelled; Hilton was the first sponsor I ever had. I still use their gyms to this day, and they're great because they're generally really quiet. They're usually only used by other hotel guests but, after the 2012 Olympics when I became more recognizable, I'd look up from doing press-ups, all sweaty and puffed out, and someone would be taking a photo of me.

Just rewinding a bit, I left school with pretty good GCSE grades and I got lots of Bs. Because I knew I wouldn't be able to make any money from boxing or get decent funding at that time, I went to study at Park Lane College. It seemed like a natural path to take while I was waiting for my boxing career to really take off. I took business studies, physical education and software and development, and carried on going to the gym as often as I could.

I didn't ever fancy the idea of going to university after sixth-form college, because I know how much work it involves and I hated the idea of not having enough time for training, so instead I went to Hopwood Hall in Middleton, Manchester, which was a sports college. It meant I could study and train at the same time, and it had loads of great facilities. I did a BTec in sports science. It was a two-year course and I'd train in between studying. It was a brilliant place, and you could do boxing, football, rugby or a civil-service course, which meant you could go on to join the army or the police. I'm so grateful to Hopwood because, at a time when women's boxing was unfunded, it was a real blessing.

The main reason I wanted to go to that college in particular was because a coach called Alwyn Belcher worked there. I knew he could make me a champion and, of course, that was my goal. I also knew that another way to achieve my dreams was to put myself in positions and situations that would enable me to do that. I had to be proactive all the time.

Alwyn has trained so many boxers and was known as

the man who made winners. I first met him at the England trials, where he was a coach for the GB men's boxing team. At first, he didn't want to train women, but I wasn't about to let that stand in my way. I had it in my head that I was going to pester him until he gave in and agreed to become one of my coaches. The good thing was that, even if I did get him to work with me, I would still be able to work with Fred, because you're allowed to have a personal coach while you work with the Team GB coaches.

I finally won Alwyn over at the European Championships in Denmark in 2007. The turning point for him was when all the other British women who were boxing went out in the first round apart from me. I won my first fight, and went on to win a silver medal that made him change his mind about working with me. He said he couldn't believe the determination I had and how often I trained. This, coupled with my performance and the potential he saw in me, made him decide to take a gamble on me.

We worked together for about eight months at Hopwood before I actually started studying there. I'd have to arrive really, really early so he had time to see me before he started work with his pupils, and it worked with us from the word go. Quite often, in the afternoon, he'd have to train other people or he'd go for a sleep, so I'd hang around and raid his video collection. I'd watch documentaries of old-school fighters like Sugar Ray Leonard or Muhammad Ali. I'd also watch videos of other amateur boxers and study their techniques so, by the time Alwyn and I had our next training session, I'd be full of ideas about new things I wanted to try.

Alwyn also had a lot of ideas of his own, and some of them were pretty unusual. He had me chopping up logs, and all sorts. Another time, I had to throw a tennis ball at a curtain for an hour in a particular way to learn how to throw an overhand right. I was thinking to myself, *Why am I doing this?*, but as soon as I put the gloves on and tried the shot it was perfect. Spot on. He also taught me a great technique for footwork using a sweeping brush, which doubles up as a great way to clean the gym. He's a clever man.

We'd sometimes train in the evening and, once Kurtis had passed his driving test, he'd drive me over to Hard and Fast and sit outside waiting for me to finish. He'd sit in his car doing his uni work for several hours, which was an amazing thing for him to do. He says now that he knew I would make it before I did. After my mum, he was my biggest supporter.

It was much easier when I started going to Hopwood Hall full time. I was kind of living in two places at that point, because I had a girlfriend who lived in Brighton, so I'd spend all week at Hopwood and at weekends I'd either go home or go to Brighton.

It's hard to say when I actually moved out of home, because I was travelling so much before I moved to

Manchester. I lived at home but I was never actually *at* home. I guess Hopwood was the first time I had my own place, and that was when I was about twenty-two, but I'd already been so independent it didn't feel like a big deal. And it helped that I lived on campus, so everything was done for us. It was a dorm of sorts, so we had meals in the dining hall and our rooms were cleaned for us.

Alwyn is a really technical coach, and that's what I needed, because I was going away to a lot more tournaments and I'd get so far and then come up against really good girls and I'd get beaten. I was fit and capable but I needed technique. He always used to tell me, 'There's no point in having the power to knock the house down if you can't hit the house.' He was full of sayings. Two of his favourites were 'Control your feet, control the bout' and 'If you're close enough to hold, you're close enough to hit.' Sometimes when you're boxing, your opponent will grab hold of you, and when I was less experienced I'd hold back or try and get them off me. Alwyn taught me that was already a good position to be in and to throw punches. That simple advice changed things a lot for me.

Alwyn is a very wise man, which is why his nickname is Mr Miyagi, after the legendary character in *The Karate Kid*. He was a boxer when he was younger, and then he became a boxing coach, so he's worked with a lot of big names, and he still loves it now, at the age of eighty-one.

He still does pads and he's got unbelievable biceps. He's super-fit and such a great coach. I'd spend two hours with him working on my technique alone, and sometimes I'd spend another two hours throwing a jab over and over again until it was right. I'd do footwork drills, which involve things like ladder drills and speed work, and shadow boxing, until they were perfect, and I guess he's made me a perfectionist.

Even when I won matches, I'd say to him, 'I could have done better,' and we'd work on the things I wasn't happy with for hours and hours. But that's what's made me the fighter I am today. I still work with him now, and I will never be able to thank him enough for all he's done for me. He believed in me, guided me, and he was tough when I needed him to be.

He's taught me how to stay relaxed and enjoy the moment when I'm in the ring and to know that my fight-or-flight mechanism won't let me down. I've learnt how to control any nerves and stay grounded. When I was younger, if I thought about a championship, I'd be nervous all day, and that uses up too much energy so I learnt good ways to switch it off. The best way to do that is to take your mind off something, and for me that means playing games or talking about anything *other* than boxing. Good-luck charms and all the rest of it can totally throw you off if something happens to go wrong with them. I would hate to rely on a pair of lucky socks or something to give me confidence.

I keep it simple so that, if something happens, like the match is running late, it's not the end of the world. I take it all in my stride. Often, one of my coaches will say, 'You're going on in five minutes,' and I'll be really surprised because I'm so engrossed in my gaming I won't have realized the time. The last thing I do before I go into the ring is chat to the coach, or coaches, who are going to be in the corner with me. We'll go through the tactics while we have a warm-up on the pads so we know we're on the same page.

When it comes to focusing, I don't sit in a quiet room with candles and white curtains or anything crazy like that. The one thing that helps my concentration is playing on my PlayStation. It helps to take my mind off things. I don't like to think about boxing all the time. I think it's too much. Some boxers on the team talk about nothing *but* boxing. They worry about the draw and who they're going to be up against, but I feel a bit like 'It is what it is. Whoever you get, you're going to have to step in the ring so there's no point in worrying about it. They're going to have two arms and two legs, so chill out!'

It's always really relaxed in my dressing room before a fight. Certain boxers are told by their coaches not to go on any social media, or they choose not to because it distracts them too much. I'm the opposite. I like seeing what's going on and keeping my fans up to date with what's happening. It's nice that they can still interact with me and almost feel like they're experiencing everything along with me.

I usually have three coaches who are there if it's just me taking part in a championship but, if there are a lot of other boxers, there can be quite a lot of people in the dressing room at once.

You get to pick who you want in your corner when you're fighting. I like a combination of someone who's serious and someone who's more relaxed and jokey. I usually have David Holloway and Lee Pullen together, because they're a great balance. Lee is the jokey character while David is more serious. The third coach is usually Gary Hale and he's a mixture of the two of them.

What I like about Dave is he'll tell you exactly how it is and there's no sugar-coating anything. If you're doing something wrong or something needs fixing, he'll tell you it was crap, and I prefer someone who tells me straight. If I'm losing in a fight, I don't want someone to say, 'Oh, it's okay, you're doing fine,' I want to know exactly what I'm up against.

I know coaches can't always be this straight down the line with every boxer they work with, because some of them don't respond very well to tough love, but it works for me. I guess it's all about people's preferences. Personally, I want the opportunity to change things and to go back out into the bout knowing what I need to do. I've always been able to take criticism and, even though he can be harsh at times, I know Dave just wants to make me a better boxer.

On the flip side, there will be times when I'm in the corner in the middle of a really serious match and I can still look down at Lee and have a laugh. I still like to have a laugh and a joke while I'm competing, because it can help to get you into a positive mind-frame, so it's good to have that combination.

As soon as the bell rings to mark the beginning of a match, I think, *Okay, down to business. Let's see how many rounds it takes to break this person down.* Sometimes you can tell straight away whether your opponent is really confident or already admitting defeat. Sometimes they'll be boxing really well but after one round they'll go back to their corner and you can look at them and know that, mentally, they've given up. You see that more with the young people who are coming up because they're not very experienced and they don't know how to handle being under pressure. They don't know what it's like to pull themselves back when they're losing. It's something you learn over time. I get over disappointment by getting better. If I don't do as well as I hoped in a match, I look at where things may have gone wrong and I improve on them. That helps me mentally, as well as with everything else.

Seasoned boxers will be focused all the way through and give you a run for your money, and to me that feels like a proper 'office day'. I call those bouts 'nine-to-fivers'. We only get one minute's rest in between rounds, so the first thing I do when I sit down in the corner is grab some water. I'm usually desperate for some because I've been sweating so much. Then whichever coach is next to you will give you a pep talk or some advice. That time is essential for getting yourself back together and taking a step back and evaluating how things are going, and that chat can make all the difference. If you're having a really tough fight, the minute you get to rest can feel like it lasts about ten seconds. But if you're doing well and you want to get back to the fight as soon as possible, it can feel like it takes for ever.

I stayed at Hopwood Hall for a few years before moving to London. I began training at a boxing gym in Haringey, and it was the perfect gym for me because I knew they did a lot for women's boxing. I worked with three coaches, called Jerry, Brian and Terri. Jerry is the owner, and he's great; Brian was the main coach, and he does pad work with boxers and goes into the corner with them; and Terri organizes tournaments and makes sure everything is in order, like checking people's boxing licences are up to date. They were a fantastic team and I always knew I'd be looked after there.

I was still training with Alwyn, but the new gym gave me other opportunities. They would pay for me to go away and compete and get me publicity, and they did a really good job of taking things to the next level. I'm still a member of the club now and I would love to go back and train there soon.

Being in London in my twenties was good fun. I had loads of friends and I did a lot of the kind of things a girl of that age would do. I was really busy with boxing, but I also went clubbing and to bars and I had a great time. I guess, in many ways, I was like any other 'normal' twenty-something. But it wasn't long before my life changed beyond all recognition.

Four:

Extra Time

Even though I'm 100 per cent focused on the match when I'm boxing, it's hard not to notice the crowd around you. When I'm competing in things like the Olympics, the noise can be deafening; sometimes, it's so intense it becomes like white noise.

It makes a huge difference if you know that the people in the crowd are supporting you. Sometimes you'll be boxing in a country where there will hardly be any British fans watching, and the atmosphere won't be the same for you. But I use it to power myself on – if everyone is shouting for my opponent, I'll think, *Right, I'm going to silence you all. If you're not cheering for me, you're not cheering for anyone.*

You can only block out so much and sometimes things will filter through, but the only time the away crowd can be off-putting is when your opponent throws a punch at you and it's nowhere near you and people start shouting, 'Yeah, good shot!' I'll be like, 'No, it wasn't! It was nowhere near me! What are you watching?'

There's nothing like having your own supporters shouting your name. If you're boxing in front of your home crowd, it's amazing. The biggest crowd I've boxed in front of was at the Commonwealth Games, where 15,000 were watching. The smallest crowds have been about 300 to 400 people, so that's quite a difference, but as long as people are behind you it lifts you.

If I've won a match, I'll be on a massive high. I'll usually go straight to do media interviews and then I'll cool down. A physio will take me through stretches to see if I've got any pains or injuries, and sometimes parts of my body will get iced to take down any inflammation. Ice is definitely the best thing if you're in pain or parts of your body are inflamed, and getting a massage from the physio helps hugely. Sadly, it's not a nice, relaxing massage with whale music and aromatherapy oils. I spend most of the treatment screaming. I swear, sometimes it's more painful than the match itself!

Sometimes it's hard to know when you've been hurt. You've got such a massive amount of adrenaline pumping round your body that, unless you've hurt something pretty badly, you just won't know. Sometimes you won't feel any pain while you're in the ring but you will afterwards, and that's a good sign because it means the injury isn't as bad as it could be. If you do feel pain somewhere during the competition, you know it's pretty bad.

I've always been really into gaming, so I thought if I was ever going to do anything else aside from boxing it would be something to do with that. I played a lot of *Super Mario* growing up, and I had a Gameboy, a Megadrive, a Nintendo 64, a Dreamcast and an Atari. These days, I love role-play and strategy games like *Final Fantasy*, *Call of Duty* and *Metal Gear Solid*. I like beat-them-up games as well, but they're a bit too simple for me. There's not much skill involved and I can win them quite quickly. I like games that are more strategic and involve skill. With strategy games, there's a consequence if you do something wrong and there's a reward if you do something right. You choose which path you want to take, and that outcome can affect the rest of the game, in the same way every decision you make can potentially affect the rest of your life. I used to watch *Dungeons and Dragons* cartoons when I was a kid and I was always fascinated by how one roll of the dice could change someone's world for ever.

Strategy games are like boxing in a way. People think boxing is a really aggressive sport and that it's about beating people up, but it's just not. In my opinion, it's not a barbaric sport at all. I see it as a work of art. There's no denying it's aggressive – at the end of the day, people are fighting and there's no sugar-coating that – but there's also a lot of skill involved. I love the technical ability that's needed – there's so much more to it than people think. It's not a case of you being able to do what you want or losing your temper and attacking someone; it's quite the opposite. If you start throwing punches randomly, that's when you could get into trouble, so you've got to be smart and you've got to be tactical. I feel terrible if I hurt someone, because that's never my goal, I just want to win. Of course, there's a level of danger involved, but you couldn't put someone who's never trained before in a ring and hope for the best. You can't just walk out and try and knock someone out, because that's not how it works. It's not about trying to hit someone as hard as you can and hoping they fall; it takes years of hard work. It's not one of those sports where you can decide you fancy giving it a go and then become a champion overnight. It takes so long to master. You can't 'play' boxing.

As I began winning more and more medals, I noticed women's boxing changing and becoming more popular. I was the only girl who was winning anything at the time, so I started getting a lot of attention. There were some other really talented girls on the British team, but they weren't as good technically as me, so I was the one who was sent abroad to fight.

We only got funding if we did well in tournaments, so we were in a real catch-22 situation. You may think, *Why bother to carry on when so much was against you?*, but the answer is, we had no choice if we wanted women's boxing to move on.

Aside from doing a paper round when I was a kid, which I hated, my mum supported me financially, as much as she could. I was busy with training, studying and helping to look after Kurtis when I was in my teens so it wasn't possible to get a proper part-time job. I really wanted to start taking the pressure off my mum but I never knew when I might get a call about a match and there aren't many places that would be understanding about you wanting to take time off at short notice.

I worked as an admin clerk in an insurance company very briefly in my late teens, which was fine, because it meant that I was always running around the office delivering things to people, which kept me sort of interested. But it still made me realize that office work wasn't for me.

When I was nineteen I was approached for a job that opened up a whole new world for me. The makers of a kids' TV series called *My Parents are Aliens* phoned my mum, because they needed a female boxer to appear on the show and have a pretend boxing match with another member of the cast. I went along for an audition and I had to do a little performance for them, but afterwards they said I looked too professional. The girl I was fighting was supposed to win the fight and they said it was unrealistic.

I'd always been keen on acting so when the producers asked if I was interested in doing more work as an extra in the future it sounded like a great idea. I signed up with an agency and started getting pretty regular work on *Coronation Street* and *Emmerdale*. The great thing about it is that you can pick and choose your hours and fit it in around what you already do.

Kurtis got into working as an extra too. He used to do parts on the same soaps as me, and he was also on

Shameless, which is funny because, if I had to best describe what my estate was like growing up, I would probably say it's more like that than anything.

It was so weird being on the *Corrie* set, because when I used to watch it I thought all the houses were real. I remember going inside one on the set and being so shocked. And they use backdrops as well so the streets look ten times longer than they actually are. The Rovers Return was tiny too. I wondered how they were going to fit us all in there (when I say 'all', I mean about ten people) when we did one scene. It was really exciting being on set and I learnt a lot about the filming side and about things you wouldn't really think about, like having to wait for a cloud to go past when you're filming a scene because it changes the lighting so much.

I spoke to some of the main actors, and they were so lovely to me. Jennie McAlpine, who plays Fizz, was really sweet and friendly, and Bill Tarmy and Liz Dawn, who played Jack and Vera, were amazing. Bill was telling me that he started off as an extra on *Coronation Street* before he auditioned for a main part, and he told me I could do the same thing.

Emmerdale was cool too and, again, nothing like I expected. But everyone was really welcoming, and all of those experiences gave me a proper taste for acting and made me think it was something I'd like to do alongside boxing.

One day, one of the producers of *Emmerdale* suggested

that I got into stunt acting, because I already had a lot of the sporting ability that's needed. He was once named the world's most prolific film and TV stuntman in the *Guinness Book of Records* and he worked on over a thousand films, including most of the James Bond movies. He was so encouraging to me and convinced me to go for it. I started doing training, which meant I had to master different disciplines. In my case, they were scuba diving, boxing (handy) and riding a motorbike. I've been able to drive a motorbike since I was ten, because my youth club took me along to kids' lessons.

I carried on acting for a long time, but when I started training for the 2012 Olympics I just didn't have the time to dedicate to it, so I had to scale it right back. But it's something I would consider going back to one day.

I missed it a lot but, luckily, I got asked to play myself in *Waterloo Road* in 2013, which was great fun. My role was to help one of the characters, Casey, build up her confidence in the boxing ring. It's another show I watched, and I spent a whole day there and the cast were amazing. I was offered an ongoing part on the show, but because boxing was taking up so much of my time, sadly, I couldn't accept.

I had to stop working as an extra altogether after the 2012 Olympics, because I was too recognizable and could no longer blend into the background. It would have been weird if people had randomly seen me in the back of shots when they were so used to seeing me box.

As well as the extra work, I got a job alongside Ray, doing house renovations. I was painting, decorating, tiling and plastering, and it really suited me. I couldn't rely on my mum for ever and I needed to do something to earn the money to keep my dream alive. I never, ever got bored of doing that job and I loved seeing a house go from being a bare shell to something amazing. It was like a real-life version of *Grand Designs* and it made me feel really proud to see how different the properties looked when they had a bit of love. It gave me a real sense of satisfaction. The great thing was that, because I was working for Ray, I could choose my own hours. As long as I got my work done, he was happy. I was training twice a day at that point so it was a lot to fit in. I'd get up at 6.30 a.m. and go for a run and go to the gym, and then I'd go to work, before heading back to the gym for another session.

Were there days when I woke up and thought, *Do you know what? Today I just can't be bothered with any of it*? Yes, there were. Sometimes I was so tired the thought of training made me want to throw the duvet over my head and hide away. But whenever that happened I focused on my opponents and the fact that they may not be having that day off. That's still what gives me the motivation to get up and out there. When you're number one, you always have someone chasing you, so I always have in the back of my mind that someone wants to take what I have.

1. Me aged two.

2. Me aged six.

3. Me aged seven with my little brother, Kurtis.

4. Me, my brother, Kurtis, and mum, Dee, on holiday in Florida.

5. Winning gold in an early boxing tournament.

6. (*left*) On the podium at the Women's World Boxing Championships in 2008.

7. A Pep-talk from my first coach, Steve Franks. He asked me if I fancied giving boxing a go and I thought, *Why not?*

8. (*above*) Training with Fred Gummerson, wearing my first 'babyface' boxing shorts that I designed myself.

9. (*right*) Training with Alwyn Belcher, aka Mr Miyagi.

10. (*above*) My proudest moment: winning the first ever Olympic gold medal for women's boxing at the London Olympic Games in 2012.

11. (*left*) My very special mum, Dee.

12. (*above*) Getting my MBE from the Queen.

13. (*right*) Posing with my brother, Kurtis, after receiving an honorary doctorate from Leeds University.

14. (*below*) Outside my postboxes in Leeds City Centre.

15. (*above*) Fighting
Sarah Ourahmoune
of France at the Rio
Olympics in 2016.

16. (*left*) Making history
again at the Rio
Olympics by winning
gold for the second time.

17. Smiling after receiving my OBE at the palace in 2017.

18. Me at the launch of my boxing collection with Everest and Selfridges.

19. One of the most important things for me, no matter what I do in the future, is to continue to inspire other women. I'm looking forward to paving the way for the next generation of professional female boxers.

When you're on top, it's hard to stay there. When some people are at the top of their game, they think they don't have to do anything else because they're already the best. But that's when people catch up to you, so you've got to be improving all the time. And you need to change things up.

There was massive pressure on me because, quite often in tournaments, I was the last British girl standing and we wanted to be able to go back to the Amateur Boxing Association of England and say, 'We're winning medals in major tournaments now. We need more funding and training camps.' I felt like it was always up to me to win a medal so we could show we were worthy. I was always fighting for so much more than medals; I was fighting for everybody. I felt like I needed and wanted to win more than anyone else in the competition because I was doing it for every woman in the UK who was either already boxing or wanted to box.

There was a lot on my shoulders. When I went into the first Olympics, one of my coaches said to me, 'Women's boxing in Great Britain needs a win or it'll be a lost cause again.' We could potentially have been pushed to the back of the queue and had our funding cut, and it was up to me to make sure that didn't happen.

As I've mentioned, I got to go to the European championships in Vejle, Denmark, in 2007, and that was the scene of one of my toughest fights to date. I was boxing against a girl called Stoyka Petrova from Bulgaria in the quarter-finals. I wanted a medal so badly, but the fight wasn't going my way. At the end of the third round, I was behind by seven points and I went into the last round knowing I had a big job to do. There aren't many times when I've nearly lost heart when I've been behind, but that was one of them, and nothing I was doing was working.

Usually, if I'm ever behind in a match, I give myself a pep talk and tell myself that I haven't put in all those hours in the gym for nothing. It's all about that moment and I *have* to find the energy from somewhere and I *have* to pull the punches. I also have to pull it out of the bag mentally. It would be easy to get frustrated in those moments, and that's when you can lose your temper or lose focus. It takes a lot of experience not to give up.

When I went over to the corner before that last round, Mr Miyagi shouted at me, 'Right, I want you to get inside and not take one step back. Just keep throwing punches. I don't care *how* you get inside but do it and *stay* there.' He was really bellowing at me, but it motivated me.

I went out into the last round, got inside, which means I'm working in short range, and I didn't stop throwing punches. I gave Petrova two standing eight counts in one round, which means you win by TKO, which is a technical knockout. That happens when the referee decides that a match shouldn't continue, but, surprisingly, I'd managed to pull back all the points anyway, and I would still have won by one point without the standing eight count. That was the first medal a British woman boxer ever won in a major tournament, so it was a really big deal. And because I'd fought through the entire tournament with a fractured knuckle, it felt like even more of a victory.

Shortly after that tournament I won a silver medal at the World Championships, which was obviously another step in the right direction. As a result, there was a big push to get women's boxing into the 2008 Olympics, and I was so excited. The bid wasn't successful, because the Olympic Committee said the standard wasn't high enough. Even though it was a huge let-down, it got people talking about women's boxing and, because of that, more girls appeared on the scene, which I was thrilled about, because it meant there were more women for me to box. That was great for a while, but then I came up against another problem – none of the other women wanted to box me. I had gained a bit of a reputation as someone who was very hard to beat and in consequence I carried on having to travel abroad to box. And due to time difference and a lack of funds, that wasn't always easy.

In November 2008 I went to the AIBA World Championships in China and, to save money, the girls' team were flown out only two days before the main tournament. There's an eight-hour time difference, so we didn't have a chance to acclimatize, but we were expected to perform to the best of our ability. I managed to get a silver medal, and I really don't know how I did it, because I was completely exhausted. I had two cans of Red Bull before the match and that just about kept me awake long enough and got me through.

Shortly after I got back from China something happened which could have potentially derailed my entire career. I was in my flat in London, packing my gym bag, ready to go to the Haringey Box Cup competition and, because I was in a real rush, I left one of my bandages hanging out. As I ran down the stairs I tripped over it and fell to the bottom. I got back up again but my back felt pretty sore so I thought I'd probably just bruised it.

I didn't think too much of it, and I made it to the competition and won, but a couple of weeks later I was still getting quite a lot of pain in my lower back. I went to hospital and they said there was nothing wrong and sent me home with some painkillers. It was only when I went to see my doctor, Mike Loosemore, who is the lead consultant in sport and exercise medicine at the Institute of Sport, and he referred me for a scan that they started investigating properly. When the results came back they discovered that I'd damaged some of the vertebrae, which meant there was no way I could fight again for a while. I was disappointed but, optimistically, I thought I'd probably be back on my feet in no time.

There was no cure other than rest – which is one of the worst things the doctors could have told me, because

I absolutely *hate* doing nothing. I was so annoyed about getting injured in such a ridiculous way. I put myself at risk every time I step into the ring and yet I'd been beaten by a bandage and a flight of stairs.

I had to wear a body cast that reached from my arm to my lower back. It was made out of hard plastic and was moulded to my body, with buckles at the front, which made it impossible to move. I had no choice but to stand up straight (when I could stand), and my mum used to joke that I'd be brilliant at finishing school. The plan was to try and get my vertebrae to mend, so I understood *why* I had the cast, but it was so restrictive. I could hardly walk a lot of the time, and I was desperate to exercise. I couldn't even go swimming because I couldn't walk to the car to drive myself to the pool.

I was given morphine patches and an oral morphine drug called Oramorph. I wore the morphine patches all the time and, as soon as they wore off, I'd wake up in the night with the pain. I used to sleep on my back with my legs curled up to my chest because it would throb constantly. I couldn't get comfortable, no matter what I did. I even tried sleeping on the hard floor to see if that would give me any relief, but it was no use.

Things got so bad I had to spend a month in hospital. I was in total agony. Although it was horrible, it was also much easier on my back, because they have the electric beds, which meant I could lift myself up. I could lower myself down and then roll over and step down to go to the toilet, which was a million times easier than having to go on my own. I never thought I'd actually *like* a hospital bed. I felt like a proper OAP. I'm surprised I didn't get a Stannah Stairlift at home.

I spent days on end lying in bed watching box sets on my laptop. I couldn't watch a normal TV. Then, to add insult to injury (quite literally), I spilt water on my laptop and it stopped working. I felt like the world had ended. A lot of the time I'd just lie there, so irritated.

I had some more tests done while I was in hospital and the doctors had to drill a hole in my back (I realize that sounds really gruesome, and it was) to make sure I hadn't done any further damage. They had to check everything to try and find out why I wasn't healing the way I should have been, but they couldn't find anything else wrong.

Eventually, the doctors suggested that I went back home for more rest, in the hope that the pain would start to ease, but even brushing my teeth took a load of effort, because I had to stand upright while I was doing it. I couldn't sit up straight because that put too much pressure on my spine, so I was barely moving at all, and I got really, really bored and quite down. I'm such a get-up-and-go person, so not being able to move and fly about like I usually do was my worst nightmare. I went from doing 300 sit-ups in a day to not being able to sit up.

My mind began working overtime and I started

thinking about what other options I had if I could never box again. I couldn't even stand unassisted, so how could I get in a ring with someone? My doctor was really encouraging and told me that the injury was in the best place it could be – any higher or lower and I would have been in serious trouble – and that I *would* get better in time. I'd never had a back-up plan, apart from maybe doing some acting, so I guess I really had no choice but to get better. I couldn't allow the fact I was feeling really low affect my future, and I had to battle really hard to stave off any feelings of negativity.

My mum was very worried about me but, because she was working and I was in London and she was in Leeds, she could only visit every so often, but she phoned me every day. Obviously, I couldn't go up and see her because I couldn't get in a car or on a train. Mum and Kurtis were a massive support and they did as much as they possibly could, but they had their own busy lives.

I started to feel really cut off and, because I didn't have anything to occupy me, the 'what if's kept trying to creep back in. It was so tough not being able to do anything myself. At times, I could barely get to the bathroom.

The fact that the doctors were so confident about my recovery was a real boost but, mentally, I was still in a bad place. It took me a long time to get my head around the fact that I couldn't do what I wanted, when I wanted. I bought an orthopaedic mattress for my flat in

London and my Auntie Myra very kindly bought me one for when I was later able to go to Mum's house in Leeds so I could be as comfortable as possible when I was there.

It's a funny thing because, even though I was lying in bed either watching TV, reading, playing my PlayStation or sleeping, I felt exhausted *all* the time because of the pain. It was so draining. I'd get muscle spasms from the top of my back right the way to the bottom because my muscles were contracting so much. When that happened I'd let out these involuntary wails and tears would start running down my cheeks. I had never felt pain that intense before and I hope I never do again. I wouldn't wish that agony on my worst enemy (not even on my toughest opponents).

It was one of those injuries that got worse before it got better, and there was nothing I could do. The Oramorph, morphine patches and muscle relaxants worked for a while but then, on top of everything else, they started to make me feel sick, so I had to start taking another drug to counteract the nausea. I was on so many tablets it started to feel normal to be completely high all the time. I honestly thought I was going to feel that way for ever, because it became the norm. I felt like I was being totally broken down and I knew that, once I did get better, I would have to work my way back up from the bottom again.

At last, my back began to heal. Every time I managed

to stand for longer than two seconds it felt like a massive achievement. Slowly but surely, I noticed that I could be upright for longer and longer, and every day felt like a bigger triumph.

As soon as I was able to travel, I went back to Leeds for a weekend. I was still feeling hugely disheartened and I needed to be around the people I loved the most. My mum gave me a proper pep talk, which basically entailed her telling me that she'd spent far too much money on my training and travel over the years for me to give up and throw it all away because of one big, but manageable, setback. Kurtis told me he had total faith that I would be able to heal fully and that it was only a matter of time before I was striking fear into every other female boxer in the world once again. They were the words I needed to hear, and I went back to London feeling so much more positive.

Once I had my body cast off, I started being able to do little bits and pieces, like swimming, and bit by bit I began to build myself back up again, both mentally and physically. Every time I achieved something new, even if it was just being able to stand up in the kitchen long enough to make myself some dinner, it made me finally feel like things were finally getting back on track.

As predicted, when I finally got back to training, I was so far away from where I'd been, and I was angry. *So* angry. I'd worked so hard for so many years and I pretty much had to go back to basics so I didn't shock my body.

The first time I was able to get back on the elliptical trainer was a massive deal for me, but I was so excited I went in a bit too hard. I did about twenty to thirty minutes and as soon as I got off I was sick because my body wasn't used to that kind of pace. I hadn't done any exercise for several months, and that taught me I had to ease myself back in, like the doctors had suggested.

I had to wait a long time to compete again, and the first major thing I did post-injury was a training camp and competition in Crete. I was sparring with some of the girls and the coaches were watching me closely to see how I was recovering. I overheard two of them say to each other that I was doing really well, and I was like, 'I'm back in the game!' As soon as I could feel myself beginning to feel like the old me again, all my determination came flooding back. It had always been there but, because of everything that had gone on, it had been pushed down. But I kept telling myself how capable I was and how well I'd done in the past, and I knew I could get back to my best again.

I sparred with the European champion and I gave her a pretty good workout. That's when I knew it was only a matter of time before I was kicking everyone's arse again.

Five:

Going for Gold

On 13 August 2009 we found out that the International Olympic Committee (IOC) was going to provide funding so that women's boxing could be included in the 2012 Olympics. At last I was going to have a chance to achieve everything I had set out to do. But my back was still playing up and, because of that, the head coach of that division of Team GB, Rob McCracken, was really nervous about me joining the squad.

I went to the English Institute of Sport in Sheffield to try out for the programme and I ended up having to sit in a chair and watch the other girls training. Rob came so close to sending me home, but Mike Loosemore begged him to give me a month to recover. The horrible reality was that if I didn't get better I wouldn't make the squad, and I was so broke I would have no choice but to walk away from boxing for ever. I started slowly, with some shadow boxing, and Rob could see my potential and took a chance on me. If he hadn't, I have no idea where I'd be now.

I had my place in the team, but now I had to qualify. Thankfully, my money troubles eased because, as soon as women's boxing became an Olympic sport, there was proper funding for a full set-up. I had physios, doctors and more coaches than I could ever need. The women's team went to training camps all over the place and it was finally how it should be. I was totally buzzing about the possibility of competing in London 2012.

I was still recovering all the time, but I had to be at peak fitness to be in with a chance of representing the UK in London. I still wasn't allowed to run because it created too much impact on my spine, but I was well enough to take part in a tournament in Crete following the earlier training camp.

I knew that my first competition back would be very much 'do or die'. If I didn't take part in that tournament, I wouldn't have been able to go to the World Championship, which would have meant I wouldn't have had a shot at going to the qualifiers for the 2012 Olympics. I was getting treatment from a physio before my first match, and she said, 'This is your one shot, and you've got to do well.' I replied, 'You fix me up and I'll do the rest.'

I ended up beating the world number one, the world champion and the European champion, all in that week. I also picked up the 'best boxer of the tournament' trophy. I still wasn't feeling 100 per cent but I thought, *If I can do that having only just recovered from a serious spinal injury, I can do anything.* London 2012, here I come!

By the time the AIBA World Championships in Barbados arrived, I was probably still only at about 60 per cent strength. I was nowhere near my full potential, but I threw everything I had into every bout. After each match, it took physios Kasia Cox and Ian Gatt for ever to loosen off the muscles in my back because they were so tight. They still weren't very strong and they weren't used to working hard so they had to be sorted out to make sure I'd be okay to compete the following day. I spent most of my time in the physio room. Sometimes I was in there twice a day for an hour each time, just so I could move around okay. I was so lucky to have such amazing physios around me. They were my saviours and, while it was a horrible situation, in the same way as my mum's illness did, it showed me how strong I can be.

Mercifully, once my back had healed, there wasn't a risk that it would go back to being as bad as it was unless I injured myself badly again. I had to be really well behaved and listen to the doctors and my coaches and not rush things (as I had been, slightly) and, fingers crossed, it's been okay ever since.

I try to look at the positive side and see the injury as a blessing, because when I came out the other side of it I was more determined than ever. The mind is so powerful. It's incredible. It has the power to both break you and heal you.

The GB selection camp took place at the Institute of Sport in late 2009 and all the boxers in the UK had to complete a fitness test and various different trials. As the camp went on, the number of people was whittled down and the ones the selection committee didn't deem to be strong enough were let go. At the very end of the camp there were only three people left in each weight division, and only one of those was going to represent the UK in the Olympics.

From that moment on, everything was based on how well you did at tournaments. Basically, if you were the boxer who was winning gold at every tournament, you would be the one who was selected. I wanted that more than I'd ever wanted anything in my life.

In November 2010, I won gold in the first ever GB Amateur Boxing Championship at the Echo Arena in Liverpool, and silver at the World Amateur Championships in Bridgetown, Barbados. The following year, I won gold at the Women's European Union Amateur Boxing Championships in Katowice, Poland, and at the European Amateur Championships in Rotterdam, The Netherlands.

It was hugely important to me that I earned valuable ranking points for the World Amateur Championships in 2012. The same year, I was named one of 'Six Promising Britons to watch in the Olympics' by the BBC, which was massively encouraging. But was I going to make it?

Because I was winning everything, I was the one flyweight female boxer who was selected to go over to China for the World Amateur Championships, which also served as the Olympic qualifiers and took place about ten weeks before the main Games. That meant I had to wait until then to discover my Olympic fate, and I kept myself busy with training and competing in the meantime.

Due to the time difference, it was decided that we'd do four weeks of training in China before the Worlds kicked off. We flew over in April 2012 and headed to Qinhuangdao to settle in. I shared an apartment with another boxer, called Savannah Marshall, who I get on really well with. There can be a bit of rivalry between boxers, but if you're not in the same weight division it isn't a problem. You would never be made to share with someone who you might have to fight. Generally, we all support each other and, even if you know your team mate is your rival, everything is determined by how well you do in competitions anyway, so, really, it's up to you.

If you're underperforming, you've only got yourself to blame. It can be a fierce environment but it's not a bitchy one because you're not being judged on how you look. You're being judged on skill and how hard you've worked, and you can't fake that.

The accommodation was very basic and Savannah and I didn't have a TV, which I was horrified about at first. But then I realized that all the channels were Chinese and everything is repeated constantly so it's not very interesting anyway. You can easily see the same programme four times in the same week. Even things like basketball matches are played again and again, even though everyone already knows the outcome. The only English-speaking channel is the news, and even that is all Chinese news.

It was hard to keep up with what was going on back home. Everything in China is so controlled, and the internet is very restricted so you can only look at certain things online. Facebook, Instagram and Twitter are banned, and there's no way round it. It was weird not being able to use social media before matches, like I usually do, but I chatted to the coaches more instead.

Much like I did when I'd visited China before, I felt like I was in a bubble while I was there and when we left and got on a plane it was a genuine shock to see British newspapers and read the news. Obviously, I was aware that there was still a world outside of China, but I'd had barely any contact with anyone and, to be honest, I felt a bit brainwashed. Unless the government chooses to report it, there's no way for you to find out about things, so I was like, 'Wow, there's other stuff going on in the world!' Not that it really matters where you are. Often places blur into one because all you're thinking about is your next match.

It's a lovely country, though. It's crazily busy and the mosquitos can be annoying, but the scenery is beautiful. I've been to the Great Wall and the Forbidden City in Beijing, and both are breathtaking. The Chinese people are amazing too. It's just a very different way of living from what I'm used to. I've been so lucky, because I've been to some really amazing places. It's a once-in-a-lifetime opportunity. Some people don't ever get to leave their own country, let alone visit the amount of places

I've been to in the world. It's one of the best things about being an athlete.

One of the big problems I had over in China was the food. The steroids they use in the meat make you test positive for steroids during drug testing, so we couldn't eat any meat at all. We were eating packet meals that were specially made for sportspeople and we had the same thing day in, day out. It was either spaghetti bolognese, jerk chicken or country chicken and rice. Imagine that on rotation for four weeks. Every day, the other athletes and I would be like, 'What have we got for lunch and dinner today? Wow, what a selection!' Luckily, I'd taken a packet of Frosties out with me so they broke up the monotony a bit, but they didn't last long.

Training was harder than ever and it involved the usual running, sparring and S&C, which stands for strength and conditioning. The Olympic Committee were only selecting four women from the whole of Europe to box in the Olympics, which was pretty daunting, when there were twelve people vying for a place. It was quite tough, and those championships turned out to be more mentally draining than the Olympics themselves because I felt like I was under so much pressure. Or rather, I put myself under a lot of pressure.

The stadium we boxed in was really nice and everything was so well organized. If you were due to box at a certain time, you'd better believe it would happen on the dot. It was never a minute earlier or a minute later. I boxed Mary Com of India in the quarter-finals, who was a five-time world champion. She was from the weight class below me but, because they had the three-weight division, she came up to 51 kilos. I knew it was going to be tough, but it wasn't actually as tough as I thought it was going to be. Because she boxes at a lower weight she was a lot smaller than I was and I totally smashed that competition.

I beat Elena Savelyeva of Russia in the semi-finals, and that meant I was guaranteed a place in the Olympics, no matter what happened in the final. I was *so* happy. Because I'd set my mind on it and held my dream since I was thirteen, I had expected to get a place. (I know it sounds arrogant, but it's true.) I didn't ever allow myself to think I wouldn't. But until someone actually tells you you're going to be taking part in the Olympics, you can't allow yourself to get too excited. Especially as I still had one big match to go, against Ren Cancan.

Cancan is without a doubt my biggest rival on the boxing circuit. We'd already boxed each other twice before, and we'd won one match each so I was desperate to beat her again. I put my all into it and I was absolutely gutted when I got silver. Cancan is from China and, although it was a very close match and I honestly thought I'd won, I think that, reading between the lines, I would have had to really blow her out of the water to get the victory. I left the World Championships so angry. So angry, in fact, I nearly threw my silver medal out of a window. Most people would think, *You've just qualified for the Olympic Games and you've scored a silver in the World Championships*, but to me all that meant was that I'd come second. And lost to Cancan. I went to China with the intention of coming home with a gold, and silver just wasn't good enough for me. I wanted it *all*. I wanted to qualify *and* I wanted a gold medal.

I'm not going to lie, I spent the next couple of weeks still feeling really angry. If anyone mentioned the Worlds or Cancan, I'd totally clam up. Usually, as soon as I've finished a tournament, I leave things behind and look forward to my next match, but this was different. It took me ages to get myself to a point when I could talk about it. I was furious.

I snapped out of it, though, and realized being angry was getting me nowhere, so I threw myself back into training and worked harder than ever. You have to pick yourself up and carry on, even when things are hard. You can either let disappointment eat away at you, or you can use it to motivate you and power you on to do better next time. I always do the latter, even if, occasionally, it takes me a little while to get there.

I only had one thing on my mind, and that was winning gold at the Olympics. In my head, that medal was already mine and no one was going to take it away from me – least of all Cancan. The Worlds made me want to show everyone that I was a champion and, even though the result was disappointing, I used it to fire me up. I told myself that the next time Cancan and I fought it wasn't even going to be close. I was going to smash it.

I noticed a big difference in the support I got when I came back from China. There was another shift, and the backing we had from the nation was unbelievable. Everyone got behind us and it felt like people had suddenly woken up to the possibility that the UK could actually be really successful in women's boxing. I started to get recognized more because we were talked about in the press and on social media, and there was definitely a big change.

I started training anything from four to six days a week, at the English Institute of Sport in Sheffield. It was pretty intense. The English Institute of Sport is a huge, really well-equipped building where all Olympic boxers train. I trained alongside the entire GB boxing team, and the atmosphere was amazing. I first began training there when women's boxing became an Olympic sport in 2009. The institute moved there from Crystal Palace, so it was more central for people travelling from all over the UK.

There's a wall as you walk into the building that's covered in photos of boxers. The only way you can make it on to that wall is by becoming a world champion or winning a medal at the Olympics. And everyone who trains there is training to become a champion. As you walk in, there's a sign on the door that reads, 'If you fail to plan, you plan to fail.' I think that says it all.

Everyone stays on site and the institute has got a strength-and-conditioning room, a physio room, doctors on call, a sauna, a jacuzzi – you name it. Everything is monitored by camera so you can watch your sparring back with performance analysts afterwards and spot any mistakes and find ways you can improve your tactics.

As soon as women's boxing started getting funding from the National Lottery, we began getting a living allowance and funding for medical bills and insurance. Because athletes who are training for the Olympics don't have time to work full-time, it's effectively like a wage. It's graded on where you're ranked in the world and the amount of medals you win. So the more successful you are, the more money you get, although, sadly, it's capped at a certain amount. I think if they didn't cap it, they'd go bankrupt, because so many GB athletes are doing amazingly well.

I'd be at training camp Monday to Thursday and then I'd go home at weekends. I'd get up at 7 a.m. and have my weight checked, run on the track for three miles from seven-thirty, then I'd have S&C mid-morning and boxing training for three hours in the afternoon. I also used to chop wood to build my upper-arm strength and, while most other people would leave the gym as soon as training was over, I would stay and carry on for as long as I could. Sometimes, the only reason I would give up was sheer exhaustion. My mind would be telling me to carry on but my body would be screaming, 'It's rest time!' Alwyn always says that's part of the reason I win.

Sometimes I had to sacrifice things during really intense training, and it could be tough. I've missed family events like weddings and christenings, but I had to make a choice early on whether I was all in or not.

We were doing longer rounds of training than usual, and more often, and I found some of the runs really hard because they were so early in the day. I remember doing the last lap once and in my head I was thinking, *Please, someone just trip me up so I don't have to do any more.* It's the interval runs I don't like. You're not going fast enough to sprint but you're not going slowly enough to jog, so it's a horrible 400-metre pace and I find it so hard. It's also judged on time, not distance, so the coaches know if you're not putting in the amount of work you should. Sometimes they'd be standing at sidelines shouting things at me like, 'Come on, Adams, pick up the pace, you might as well be running backwards!' 'Shall we just get you a bus for the next lap?' 'Why are you at the back with the super-heavies?'

I enjoy strength training most because I enjoy weight lifting, and of course I love boxing sessions. The coaches motivate you with tough love so there is a lot of shouting involved but, as I've said before, I can take it.

No two boxers have the same workout so, aside from running, you generally do everything on your own. Because we're all in different weight categories, our programmes are tailored to us by a strength-and-conditioning coach. Your regime also changes if you've got an injury or you're recovering from one, or if the coaches want you to strengthen a certain part of your body.

Every summer and at the end of every year the entire boxing team have an extensive fitness test so the trainers can see where you're strongest and where you're weakest. Then they'll modify your programme accordingly. It might be that one of your legs is stronger than the other, so you have to concentrate on building the weaker one up, or you may need more core strength.

I was feeling good in the run-up to the Olympics. I focused my pre-Games, ten-week training camp on facing and beating Cancan, and I felt really positive. My weight was right, I was fit and I was ready for her. She was ranked number one in the world and I was ranked number two, but things weren't going to stay that way for long.

I was so happy the Olympics were based in the UK that year. It was the first time women's boxing was making an appearance in the Olympics and we were doing it on home soil.

The atmosphere across Britain was incredible from the minute summer kicked off. The excitement levels were off the chart. It felt so good. Even when I travelled on the Tube, people were smiling and happy, which rarely happens in London. I went to stay in the Olympic Village in Stratford, east London, two weeks before the Games began, and it was such a cool place. It's really well set out, and so big there were red buses driving around so you could hop on and off at different food halls. Once you were inside the village, you weren't allowed to come and go as you pleased, so it was a little bit restrictive. If you wanted to leave, you had to get permission from the coaches, so it was quite a strict set-up, but then again, you had everything you needed on site.

I shared a room with Savannah again, in the main GB house, and another boxer, Natasha Jonas, had her own room in the same flat. The flat was quite small and had two bedrooms, a bathroom, a kitchen and a living area. It was simple, but it did the job. There was a big barbecue dining area in front of the GB house, which, obviously, I loved. Everything was cooked freshly on a grill and they had good music playing. There was also an inside food court that was *huge*. It had a McDonald's, Far Eastern food, Italian – you name it. And it was all free. You just had to show your ID on the door and you could go in and help yourself. We were also given swipe cards to use in the vending machines so we could get drinks and snacks whenever we wanted them.

It was brilliant, but also hard at times, because I was in full-on health mode and couldn't eat everything I wanted to. In the evenings, they had these amazing cakes laid out in the British dining area, so Savannah and I would wait until the coaches had left for the evening and then sneak up and get one each.

The Olympics opening ceremony on 27 July was every

bit as mind-blowing as it looked on TV. I was totally stunned, and the whole scene with the Queen and James Bond where 'she' jumped from a helicopter was breathtaking. To be there and be a part of it was ... I can't really describe it. Whatever I was expecting, it was ten times better. Walking into the crowds of people who were shouting and screaming was unbelievable, *and* the Spice Girls were there.

Everyone in the village was really upbeat and there was always someone to talk to. There were a few times early on in the Games when the GB team got a bit despondent because we weren't winning any medals. But as soon as we got our first one – a silver medal won by Lizzie Armistead in the women's road cycling race – everyone's spirits lifted. There was a medal chart on the wall in the Team GB house, along with a counter, and every time we won something it was added to the tally.

I spent most of my time in the village training, but when I had downtime I was watching TV and playing on my PlayStation. So it wasn't much different from what I did at home, really. I had to wait a couple of weeks for my first match, and I just wanted to start boxing. I was desperate for my Olympic journey to begin.

The day before the competition kicked off, officials had done a draw, so I knew who I was up against in my flyweight category. It was Stoyka Petrova, who I'd beaten six times before, so I felt confident. I kept thinking, *She's unlucky to draw me!* It went as well as I'd hoped, and I won.

Because there are certain girls who are really good, you can pretty much guarantee that they're the ones who will be in the semis and the finals of any competition. The same five tend to be up there and, because of that, I often box the same girls over and over. It's like how you always know Andy Murray, Roger Federer and Rafa Nadal will always be at the top of the big tennis championships. Certain athletes will always be facing off against each other.

I fought Mary Com again in the semi-finals and won, and because Cancan had also won her matches, it was going to be me and her going head to head in the final. I couldn't wait.

Every time I did an interview in the lead-up to the final I told the reporter how much I wanted to beat Cancan. I wanted the opportunity to claim my crown. There is genuine rivalry there. We have a mutual respect for each other and we know we're both good opponents, but we won't be sitting down for a coffee together any time soon.

Weirdly, I felt okay the night before the match, and I got to sleep pretty easily. But then I woke up at around 4 a.m. and that was it – I couldn't get back to sleep, no matter what I did. I started thinking about tactics so my brain was ticking over, and every time I closed my eyes I'd think about how much I wanted to win the final.

I had to be up at 6.30 a.m. for the weigh-in so I gave up and got up and had some breakfast. Then I went back to bed. Thankfully, I managed to have a small nap before I got dressed and did my weigh-in.

I knew I was physically ready but I had to get myself mentally prepared. That's half the battle. I visualize winning and I think about the tactics I'm going to be using, and that gets me in the right frame of mind. I've seen people win a match before they even step into the ring, so you have to be in the right headspace. I spent a good amount of time talking to my coaches in the dressing room beforehand, and I also reminded myself that I was more than capable of walking away with a gold medal that day.

The match wasn't until 4.30 p.m., so I had a long wait, but when I finally stepped into the ring I thought, *This is my time.* The noise from the crowd was deafening and I used it as a motivator.

I was waving at the crowd and shadow boxing and doing the Ali shuffle, and I loved every moment. I looked over at Cancan to see if she was up for the job or not. I can tell by looking in someone's eyes how long it will take for me to break their confidence. I could see she was determined, and I was like, 'Bring it on!' The atmosphere was so uplifting I felt like I was floating. I planned to draw in all of the energy and use it to my advantage.

The bell went and I was straight into the tactics. Everything was going so well it almost felt like it was going *too* well at some points, and I felt like I was winning the match quite easily. I really didn't expect that, because it had been really, really close in every match Cancan and I had fought until then.

I went back to the corner, to my coaches David Holloway and Paul Warmsley, and they said to me, 'Right, you're in front but you're only two points up,' and I thought, *How can I be? I thought I was way ahead?* They told me to stay focused and *win* and as I went into the second round I could feel everything was going my way. I scored a knockdown and I was like, 'YES!' The crowd went absolutely wild and, after that moment, I was like, 'Yeah, I've got this.' Cancan got back up and, because she was so frustrated, she played right into my hands. She was still a dangerous opponent but, in that moment, I knew I had it.

Cancan started coming forward towards me, and that isn't her strength at all. She's a counter puncher and she likes to stay on her back foot and move around the ring. But because I was winning she had to go forward to be in with a chance of beating me.

When the match ended, I knew I'd won but I didn't realize by how many points – nine – until it was announced. Apparently, the noise in the arena when I won was equivalent to a jumbo jet taking off, so I think it's safe to say the home crowd was happy.

It turned out my coaches had lied to me about how far ahead I was after the first round. They didn't want me to become too sure of myself and they needed me to continue working my hardest. They made me think there was still a good chance I could lose so that I fought with everything I had. It was a good game plan on their part.

That moment when I realized I'd won gold isn't something I can articulate. I'd won the *Olympics*. I was the first women's Olympic boxing champion *ever*.

It's usually only China, Russia or the US that wins those kinds of trophies but this time it was *ours*. I felt like I'd come *so* far from not being able to afford to go to tournaments and not being allowed to share a gym with the men's boxing team to standing in a ring having just made history. There were people in the audience crying their eyes out, and I felt so proud. It may sound a bit cheesy but I was as excited for the rest of the country as I was for myself. It was such a fairy-tale ending.

To have done such an amazing thing for all those people who had turned out to support me felt unbelievable. My friends and family were in the arena watching me, and it was only afterwards I found out that there were royals in the crowd. Even the then prime minister, David Cameron, came to watch. So many people were trying to get tickets, because everyone was desperate to watch the match, and my mum said she was offered tons of money for hers. (She knows I would have killed her if she'd sold them.)

Can you imagine how good it feels after all those years of not being supported or believed in? That day showed me that anything is possible. If you believe in yourself and don't let anyone or anything stand in your way, you can achieve anything you want to.

I don't know what went wrong for Cancan during that match. To put it simply, I was . . . better. I'd spent so much time focusing and watching videos of her boxing, so I had her worked out to a T. I felt like I knew her inside out. There is no reason she should ever beat me again.

I didn't realize until I watched the fight back afterwards what an amazing bout it was. Everyone was talking about it, and so many people contacted me to tell me how much they loved it and that it had opened their eyes to something new – women's boxing.

To be fair to her, Cancan took the defeat pretty well, but I didn't see her compete for about another two years. When she did come back she'd changed her style a little bit. I like to think it was because she'd been sat in a room with the walls covered in photos of me, watching videos of all our matches, which, to be fair, is exactly what I would have done if things had been the other way round. I would have been absolutely devastated if I'd won silver. Imagine having to wait a whole four years before you can challenge that person again.

I didn't get to see my family until around midnight on the day I won because things were so crazy. I did a lot of media interviews after my win and then I went straight into anti-doping. During tournaments, all of the gold medallists have to go through testing, and the silver medallists are tested at random.

Anti-doping involves having to give blood and urine

samples and it always takes me forever to go to the toilet, especially because you've got someone sitting there watching you to make sure you don't cheat and switch samples (yep). Clearly, there's zero privacy, but I feel just as bad for them as I do for me. It can't be much fun.

It's funny because people probably expect me to have performance anxiety when I'm fighting but, actually, it happens afterwards, when I'm sat with a random woman holding a clipboard willing me to pee. I did drink loads and loads of water but, because I'd been sweating so much in the ring, it took me ages. I was so desperate to see my friends and family and go, 'YAAAAAAAY!' but instead I was sat in front of this poor woman, hoping I could perform in a totally different way.

I was sat there for four hours in total, and that's actually quite good for me, because if I'm *really* dehydrated it can take me about six hours to go. Every time I walk into an anti-doping room I look at the woman who's going to be monitoring me and think, *You'd better get comfortable, because this is going to be a* long *night.* After the 2012 World Championships it took me eight hours to wee. The woman kept shouting at me in Chinese (I think telling me to go to the toilet) so it was really off-putting and, even though I wanted to go, I couldn't.

There was quite a lot of partying going on in the village, but I was always so busy with media and interviews I didn't get a chance to join in. Even after the closing ceremony, when I should have been celebrating my win,

I was so tired all I wanted to do was sleep. I did have a few drinks afterwards, and they put alcohol in the vending machines so there was easy access to it, but all I wanted was a McDonald's and my bed.

The closing ceremony was every bit as brilliant as the opening ceremony. It was an incredible way to round out what had been a totally life-changing month. We all felt so proud of Team GB and we were all so happy for each other. I honestly wish I could go back and do it all again.

Six:

Pretty Fly

Once I left the Olympic village I headed back to Leeds to have a celebratory dinner with my family. I'd love to say we all got dressed up and went to some really posh restaurant, but we went to Nando's and it was perfect.

I couldn't believe the reaction I got after 2012. I did so many interviews, it was non-stop. I was driving back and forth to London and I was still boxing and training as much as possible, so things got so busy I barely saw my family. I thought maybe I'd get a bit of attention following the win, but I was not expecting what came my way. I remember thinking that I'd still be able to go to the supermarket and do my shopping, like I always had, but even getting a pint of milk would take half an hour and, one day when I went to the supermarket, I had to ditch my trolley and security had to help me out of the store. Things have settled down, but I'm more mindful now and I'll either go to a twenty-four-hour supermarket at about 2 a.m., or I shop online.

I've never done the whole VIP thing on a night out, but suddenly I found that when I went clubbing I had to go into private sections so I could get some space to see my friends. It was very different, not being able to just roam around a club. I never thought I'd be the kind of person to use a VIP area, but I do understand now why clubs have them. I get that it can just be easier, and it's not all about getting the chance to pose and think you're really important. I'm sure there is an element of that with some people, but I do it purely so I can chill with my friends for a bit. If there's a big group of us going out, sometimes we'll even call a venue up and see if they can sort out an area for us. When people are drunk, it magnifies everything and there's no filter, so people don't just want a selfie, they want to talk to you for ages and ask loads of questions and take a hundred photos. That's totally cool until you realize you've been in a place for three hours and you haven't had a chance to get a drink. I suppose it's just about being sensible and trying to live as normal a life as possible. I haven't gone as far as taking bodyguards out or anything – I think that's a bit extreme. I've never had anyone trying to fight me after a few drinks either, thankfully. I think it tends to happen more with the boys. I know some male boxers it's happened to.

I do get grabbed sometimes, and it's fine when there are a couple of people, but when there are more it can be quite scary. It can be that someone just wants a hug, but if I'm walking down the street and someone comes up and gives me a cuddle I do feel quite taken aback. Often people think they know you because they've seen you on TV, so they're not afraid to approach you. But think how weird it would be if you went up to someone you've never met before and started hugging them. My mum says it's because I come across as too nice. Maybe I need to start being grumpier during interviews.

It was strange at first, being recognized so much, and it was also quite tiring at times because I was having so many selfies taken it felt like I was working on a night out instead of having a laugh with my mates, so I had to try and find a balance. I'm always happy to sign autographs for people and let them take selfies. I know some people find it a bit annoying, but the person that comes up to you is excited and they're not thinking about the fact that they may be the twentieth person to approach you that day. They just want to say hello and chat, and it is a part of what I do, in a way, so I try to accommodate people as much as possible. I would hate to have to say no to anyone who wants to say hello, so now I do factor in extra time if I am going out. The nation supported me when I was in the Olympics and I'll be forever grateful for that. It's so funny because, sometimes, parents will send their kids up to talk to me because they're too embarrassed to come over themselves. Other people will stare or whisper. Then you have the people who randomly shout your name out when you're walking down the street. I find that hilarious.

The weirdest place I've been spotted is in the changing room in a clothes shop. I was talking to my friend, who was in the next cubicle, and this woman knocked on the door and said, 'Are you Nicola Adams?' I was so impressed that she recognized me from my voice alone that, despite being halfway through getting dressed, I had to go out and have a selfie taken with her.

Things also changed for my friends and family. They wanted to spend time with me, and it was hard to have a proper conversation if we were out because people would want to talk to me. There have been times when a friend or family member has said no to people on my behalf because they want to have a proper chat. One time I was in the middle of something so a friend of mine said to this lady, 'I'm so sorry, Nicola can't do a photo just at the moment,' and this woman replied really angrily, 'You're not sorry!' I felt terrible! My friends are great and they know that, sometimes, if we go somewhere, it will be a bit of a mission and everything needs to be planned really precisely. They're the ones who'll take charge.

There were certain times when I would think it's easier to just stay in, and if I need some butter or something I sometimes wait for my brother to come home and bring me some rather than venturing out. When I buy petrol, I'll go to a station where you can pay at the machine, because if I have to go into the shop I can be in there for ages and it's tricky if I'm in a rush. Please don't think I'm complaining about being recognized, because I'm not. Most of the time I think it's cool, but I guess everyone has those days when they want to hibernate a bit.

Sometimes I'll go out wearing a hat and glasses as a

bit of a disguise, and sometimes it works and sometimes it doesn't. Even if I'm in a cap and sunglasses, I'll see people do a bit of a double-take, so I think I must also have quite a recognizable face. Or maybe I'm not very good at disguises? I used to take being able to walk around unnoticed for granted and I do miss it sometimes, but I wouldn't change what I've achieved for anything.

In the December following the Olympics I decided to go on holiday to Mexico so I could have a break and get away from everything and recharge. I was so excited, but when I got to my hotel I realized that the World Boxing Council had decided to hold their yearly conference in the hotel I was in. Of all the places in the world, it happened to be there, so the hotel was full of boxing fans. I was like, 'Are you kidding?' Mum phoned me and said, 'How's your holiday? I bet you're having a lovely break from everything?' and I replied, 'Yeah, there are tons of boxing fans here! What are the chances?'

The other thing that changed in my life was the massive press interest. But not just in my boxing career, in my private life too.

A few of my friends were asked questions about me and reporters started turning up on my mum's doorstep. I couldn't work out how they knew where she lived until someone told me they have access to everyone's address. That really shocked me. I didn't get asked anything too bad personally, though. Most of the interviews I did were quite sport-based but now they've shifted a bit and I will get asked about relationships and my family. I also get asked quite random questions. For instance, if someone gets sacked from somewhere or there's a big scandal, I'll get asked for my opinion on it. I guess, because I do what I do, there will be times when people write things I'm not that happy about, but I take it with a pinch of salt. There's no point in getting upset by things, because you can't control everything, no matter how hard you try. I rarely read or watch interviews I've done because I think it's weird. As soon as I've done an interview I walk away and forget about it.

I've been really lucky with social media because I don't get trolled and I would say that 99.9 per cent of the comments are positive. The ones that aren't I don't care about. If I do read something negative, I have to remind myself that the person writing it is just someone who is sat on the other end of a computer and they're probably quite unhappy. I think if you take time out of your day to say something negative to someone, you can't be a very positive person. If you had a lot going on and you felt good about yourself, you wouldn't feel the need to attack a total stranger for kicks. There's no way those people would ever come up and say the things they say online to my face. And I guess it's still flattering, in a way. At least someone has still spent their time going on to your Twitter page to tell you something, whether it's bad or good. It's still love.

Thankfully, because I'm a strong personality, none of the changes to my life really affected me that much. I know myself really well and I didn't ever think, *Oh, brilliant, I can go to Sugar Hut every night and spend tons of money on designer clothes and be a celebrity*, because that's just not who I am. I didn't want to change, so I didn't and I never will. I've had the same friends for years, but I had all sorts of people creeping out of the woodwork after 2012. I had cousins I'd never even heard of contacting me, and my Facebook requests were crazy. There were people I hadn't seen since school, and maybe didn't even know at school, asking to be my friend. It felt like once I was in the spotlight, everyone wanted to be a part of it.

Probably the most shocking thing for me was that my dad turned up at the Olympics. I hadn't seen him for a while beforehand – his appearances throughout my life have always been pretty random – and all I could think was, *How dare you! You've been absent for most of my life and then you appear out of nowhere and make out that you've been there the whole time?* I was so angry.

The only saving grace was that I didn't know he was watching the fight until afterwards. Imagine if I had been halfway through the match and then I'd looked out and seen him? It could have fired me up and made me more determined, or it could have gone the other way and completely put me off. I think his actions were selfish, especially as he didn't give me any warning. He wasn't thinking about what kind of effect him being there might have on me, he was just thinking of himself.

He came to the friends and family room in the Team GB house the following day and we had an awkward 'hi', but that was it. There was no conversation or anything, and I haven't seen him since that day, funnily enough. I think he wanted the glory, and then he was off again. It may also be because I did make it clear I wasn't happy that he was there.

I got a good-luck text message from him before I took part in the Rio Olympics as well. I'd been taking part in tournaments for the entire four years since 2012 and he hadn't wished me luck for any of those, but I think that as soon as something major came up he wanted to be a part of it again. In my opinion, he only wants to be there for the good times, which I find annoying. I felt like, *How dare you just want to be there for the exciting stuff!* He's remarried, and I hope he's happy, but I don't want to be a part of his life. You never know, that might change, but right now I don't have any interest in seeing him.

My life has never really gone back to 'normal' since 2012. It was a game-changer, and the only things that have stayed constant in my life are the people close to me and my training. I still see the same people in the gym I always have and they don't care about what I have and haven't done. They treat me the same as they always have. I'm just Nikki to them, medals or no medals.

I do think having the same people around me makes a

difference. I can see how people get swept up in the excitement of being famous, or however you'd describe what I am now. But if I ever tried to throw any diva strops (aside from being grumpy about not winning a tournament), my mum and my brother would put me straight back in my place. My brother, in particular, still takes the mickey out of me all the time. Our relationship hasn't changed at all. We live together, and I still have to make cups of tea when people come round, and do the washing-up.

I started doing a lot of photoshoots and interviews post-2012. I really like fashion, so getting to do a photoshoot for *Vogue* was right up my street. It was really exciting and I loved being around all the beautiful clothes. Everyone was very friendly and cool, and when I saw the photos I was like, 'Wow, is that me?' I always wish I could do my make-up like professional make-up artists do.

I've also done some modelling, and that's something else I've loved. I did a campaign for Panache in 2016 and I worked on Marks and Spencer's 'Britain's Leading Ladies' campaign in 2013, alongside incredible women like Ellie Goulding, Katie Piper and Dame Helen Mirren. I was totally in awe of Helen and when she told me that she was a big fan of mine and she watches my matches I was blown away.

I love wearing a good suit, and I love good shoes and bags. They're a bit of a weakness. I always wait for the new Jimmy Choo collections to come out so I can get some cool trainers. My usual go-to shops are Selfridges or Harrods and, in terms of brands, I love Alexander McQueen, Phillip Lim and Helmut Lang. And, keeping things simple, I like Nike too. When I was growing up and having to decide whether to go on a training camp or buy a new pair of shoes, I didn't ever imagine I'd be wearing all these amazing things. It makes me realize how far I've come and how much I've achieved.

I also got to do really cool things like go to movie premieres. I'd never done that kind of thing before, but all of a sudden I was being invited to these glamorous events. The first premiere I went to was *The Twilight Saga: Breaking Dawn – Part 2*, in November 2012. It was a really big one, because they took over most of Leicester Square, and I got to meet all the cast, which was brilliant.

I don't know what I was expecting, but it wasn't how I thought it was going to be. When you see premieres on TV you only see a little bit of the red carpet and the actors walking up to greet the fans, but this was crazily big. It was weird when we watched the film because you're in a cinema with a load of other people, like you always are, but that time, the audience were pretty much all famous.

I was awarded an MBE (Member of the Order of the British Empire) in 2013 and, needless to say, that was an incredible moment – although the thing my mum was most concerned about was what to wear. She was terrified people were going to ask her where her outfit was from, like they do on the red carpet, and she wasn't going to be able to say it was designer. Luckily, I had a stylist who helped me decide what to wear because, otherwise, I probably would have worried too.

Mum was also very concerned when she was told that she had to either wear a hat or a fascinator. She had no idea what a fascinator was. She thought she was going to have to dress up in a ridiculous suit or something, and she was so relieved when she found out that, in her words, 'It's just an Alice band with something stuck on it.' She ended up borrowing one from a friend, but she's promised herself that if she ever gets to meet the Queen again she's going to buy herself some kind of amazing hat.

I went to Buckingham Palace with my mum, Kurtis and my Uncle Robert, and we all spent the night before in a hotel in central London and arrived at the Palace really early, on 28 February 2013. Mum was anxious about being late and it was a freezing-cold day, so we decided to have a walk around the gift shop. It was a bit surreal, looking at commemorative pens and mugs, when I was due to go into the Palace and meet the Queen any minute.

I've met her about five times now, but I'll never get used to being in the same room as her. I get nervous in case I do something wrong or don't follow the correct procedures. You're not allowed to speak to her until she speaks to you and you have to curtsy, and I'm always worried I'll forget something.

In October 2016, all the Olympic medallists got to go to Buckingham Palace and meet the royal family, and that was also an amazing day. Strangely, I don't get nervous about seeing Kate and William, because I know that they follow the Olympics and the boxing closely, so I've always got something to talk to them about.

On top of the MBE, I was awarded an honorary doctorate by Leeds University in 2015, so I instantly became ten times smarter. I can now call myself Dr Nicola Adams MBE. That's a pretty cool title, and one my mum is crazily excited about.

Then, at the end of 2016, I got some even more amazing news when I got a letter in the post telling me I'd been awarded an OBE. I had to keep it confidential until the New Year's Honours list was announced. I was really happy and excited when I got the letter. It was like the icing on the cake of a brilliant year. I was so proud and honoured to collect my OBE in early March 2017. I got the chance to go back to Buckingham Palace to receive it from the Duke of Cambridge for my services to boxing. I am now officially an Officer of the Most Excellent Order of the British Empire, and my mum got herself a great fascinator to wear for the day, which she was very pleased about.

I've been to some really great events since 2012, but I'm not the kind of person who would go to anything they're invited to. I don't understand how people have time. The 2016 MOBOs in Glasgow were amazing, because I usually go along to the event to present awards, and that time I was receiving the Paving the Way award. I didn't think I'd ever get one, and I used to look at them and think, *I'd love one of those.* And the fact I got one for giving girls a path to follow into sport meant so much.

I really do feel like there's a path for young female boxers to follow now and, hopefully, they won't have to struggle and worry about funding. They'll see that there's a way. I really hope that because girls have watched me achieve the things I'd dreamed of they now know they can do the same.

The *GQ* awards in 2016 were ridiculous – there were so many big celebrities there, like Chris Pine and Calvin Harris. I don't really get star-struck, but it's great to meet new people. I was really happy to meet The Rock, because he's a big boxing fan. He told me his dad used to spar Ali in his younger years, which is a great fact. The only person I've ever been star-struck by was Sugar Ray Leonard. I met him at a boxing dinner and I got to sit down and chat to him the whole evening. We spoke about what it was like when he was boxing. Back then, they didn't have nutritionists or strength coaches, or anything like that. There wasn't much science involved in boxing in those days, and it was so interesting to hear what things were like. If Sugar Ray was trying to lose weight before a match, he'd sit in his car with loads of bin bags wrapped around him so he could sweat any excess water out. It must have been so uncomfortable. These days, we use saunas to take off water weight and it's amazingly effective. If I sit in the sauna for twenty minutes I can easily lose a kilo. It's a quick fix – as soon as you drink water again it all goes back on – but at least it works in the short term.

Boxing isn't what you'd call glamorous, and you do have to be so careful with food before a match. Sometimes, the day before a tournament, I'll have a grapefruit for breakfast and a piece of chicken in the afternoon, and then I can't drink anything until I weigh in at seven o'clock the following morning. I have to carry on training as well, and I may have to go into the sauna for a big session knowing I can't drink any water afterwards. I'll be walking around thirsty, hungry and angry, thinking, *I can't wait to box, so I can eat a proper meal*. Sometimes I go to bed really early just so I don't have to put up with wanting to eat and drink so badly. There have been a couple of times where I've had a dream that I've drunk water and I've shot up in the night having a massive panic that I'm going to be over my weight in the morning. That's such a horrible feeling. I must be so desperate for a drink it's preying on my mind.

I get weighed right before I go to bed to make sure I'm on track for the weigh-in, and I know I lose half a kilo in my sleep, so if I'm slightly over I'll be bang on the right weight in the morning. It's so specific.

You realize the joys of the simple things when you're finally able to have a glass of water again after abstaining for so long. Once you weigh in, you still can't go too crazy with food and drink, because if you're boxing the following day you'll only have to try and get the weight off again, so the struggle continues. If I'm boxing in the afternoon, I'll have breakfast and lunch, then I'll compete, and after that I'll usually be about a kilo and a half over my weight. I'll skip off a kilo, and I won't have anything else to eat or drink the following day. Sometimes that means not eating or drinking anything else from 2 p.m. until 7 a.m.

When you see boxers who don't follow a regime properly it really hits home why you do it. There are some boxers who find it really hard to discipline themselves. They'll be on weight one minute and they'll come back for the check weight before the match and they'll have put on almost a kilo in two hours. There's then a small two-hour window for you to try and lose it by training; if you don't, you won't get to enter the competition. You're automatically out just because you've eaten and drunk more than you should.

Even if they do get the weight back off, because they've had to put in so much effort to lose it, they'll have nothing left to give in the competition. They're sharp for a couple of seconds and then their energy fades to nothing. It's only really the super-heavy-weights that can eat what they want, so usually everyone else taking part in a tournament is being really strict. If you want to win, you have to be strict with yourself.

I step up my focus on everything in the run-up to a championship, including my diet. But I'll be honest, I do eat rubbish in between. I'm not a saint, and there are plenty of times when you'll find me sitting on the sofa with a takeaway. I really like food, and I don't deprive myself when I don't have to, but when I'm in proper training I'll cut that out and get back to being healthy. It's a weight-controlled sport, so you don't want to balloon to some ridiculous weight and then have to work crazily hard to get it all off again. Even for someone like me, who exercises non-stop, the weight can be hard to get off when you need to.

When I'm training, I often have all my meals delivered, so they're already pre-prepared for my weight. I might have a chilli con carne or jerk chicken with rice and vegetables or soup. They're really balanced, and that does help me to stay on the straight and narrow. It can be annoying when I get a meal I'm not keen on delivered, though, because then all I can think of is Nando's.

If I'm not having meals delivered and I'm training, I'll have either egg on toast or porridge for breakfast. For lunch I'll just have chicken, vegetables, with a little bit of carbs, maybe rice or pasta. I normally have steak with vegetables in the evening, and I won't eat carbs after 7 p.m., because your body tends to store them as fat. I still let myself have treats when I'm training because, otherwise, I'd end up pigging out, so every now and again I'll have ice cream, a slice of pizza, some biscuits or a muffin. It's safe to say I've got a bit of a sweet tooth.

I do feel a massive difference when I eat well. I know

my body so well, and I can sense it's not working as well if I'm not putting good things into it. And the good thing is, when I'm at training camps, I'm always so closely monitored I couldn't cheat even if I wanted to. You're weighed every morning and our weights are written up on a board. If it's written in green, you're in line with what your weight should be, but if it's in red, you've got a bit of work to do. You're checked constantly to ensure you haven't gone too far over, or under, what you should be. I weigh myself at home too, just to keep an eye on things and make sure I don't get a shock when I step on professional scales. The exercise I do does help to keep my weight steady, but I have to stay within 5 per cent of my weight, so I can't be more than 53.6 kg at any time. It doesn't take a lot to put on weight once you're not being as active as usual, so I can't suddenly decide to take a month off and just hope for the best.

I realize that some people may not think I have the stereotypical 'female' body, but I'm very lucky because I've never had body-image issues. I love my muscles and I love looking fit, and sweating makes me feel good. The only time I don't like to sweat is when I'm on the dance floor in a club, but when I'm boxing I feel like the more I sweat, the better.

Because I had more of a profile after 2012, I was able to get more involved with charity work. I had already done some work with the Teenage Cancer Trust and I also got involved with an incredible charity called Fight for Peace.

I went out to Rio for a weekend in September 2012 with prime minister David Cameron to visit the charity, and I absolutely fell in love with it. Fight for Peace helps kids from disadvantaged backgrounds, as well as those who are affected by crime and violence, get into sport. It helps them to get into education so they can, hopefully, go on to find jobs. The hope is that we can help young people create positive futures for themselves.

It was so sad because while we were there all these kids were drawing pictures for us. Usually when you see children's drawings they're full of sunshine and green fields and parents holding hands, but the pictures they were drawing were of people shooting other people from helicopters. It's so awful to think that a five-year-old has witnessed something like that.

The charity does such incredible, positive work, and it's amazing getting to see what a difference they make to people's lives. I saw one guy completely turn his life around. He used to be in gangs and he was a major drug dealer. Fight for Peace offered him help and now he's left it all behind and he's getting an education and he's started boxing. He didn't have any kind of education because he was born into such a destructive lifestyle. In some ways, he didn't stand a chance, but now, thanks to the charity, he's been given one.

The people who work for the charity are so inspiring. Every day, they're risking their lives by going into the favelas, the Brazilian slums, to help the people living there. The gangs that run the favelas don't want people getting involved in the areas they control, so it's incredibly dangerous. It's like something out of a film.

It was very cool working with David Cameron. I got on really well with him and the trip was such an experience. David is a big boxing fan and, of course, he'd seen me fight during the Olympics, so we talked about that for a while, as well as the work the charity does.

I flew out to Rio on a regular chartered flight but when we flew back we were running late for our flight and I was thinking, *Oh, no, we're going to miss it. I wonder when the next one is.* Then, when we got to the airport, I realized that we were travelling on David Cameron's private plane. It wasn't a swanky jet with massive seats and free-flowing champagne, like you see in music videos. It was just a normal plane – apart from the fact that fighter jets fly alongside it. That wasn't *quite* so normal.

Two years ago, Fight for Peace asked me if I wanted to be an ambassador for the charity. It was a real honour. I've been working closely with them ever since. I don't want to sound clichéd, but it does feel amazing to give something back and to be able to work with people so they can have their voices heard. It's great to know that you can help other people. It's such a worthwhile charity, and it's grown now, it's worldwide, which is amazing to see.

Seven:

Real in Rio

I had a few months off from really hardcore training after 2012 because I had to have an operation on my right hand. I injured it competing in the World Championships, so when I was boxing in the Olympics I was having an anaesthesia injection to completely numb the pain about an hour before every match. It would take away the pain for a while and then, straight after the competition, the physios would compress my hand and put ice on it to take the swelling down so I was ready to fight again the following day. There wasn't enough time for me to have the operation in between the Worlds and the Olympics; I had to wait until I had a decent length of time so it could heal properly.

The operation involved doctors repairing the cartilage in my knuckles, and it was very painful afterwards. I have a tendency to move in my sleep and one night I dreamt I was doing pad work and I punched a wall. It was so sore. Because of that, I had to start tying my right arm around my neck every night when I went to bed so I didn't do the same thing again.

I was cleared to start proper training again five months after the operation, and the first thing I did was throw some punches on a water bag, which wasn't very sensible. My hand was really oversensitive, so I had to build things up slowly. For the next five months, I had to get used to hitting heavier and heavier stuff until my hand strengthened up again.

I wasn't allowed to compete at all until my hand had fully healed, so the next competition I took part in was the European Unions in July 2013. I won gold there, so I was happy. I took loads of time out and came back and still destroyed everybody.

After 2012, I knew what my next step was going to be, and that was to go for gold at the Rio 2016 Olympics. There had never been a double Olympic boxing champion before and I wanted to be the first one. I also wanted to win the World Championships and the Commonwealth Games. They became my new ones.

Some people write their goals down, but I hold mine in my head. I've never learnt any focusing techniques as such, although I have worked with sports psychologists who teach visualization. They also teach self-confidence but, as you can probably tell, I've never suffered much in that area. Funnily enough, because I do naturally most of the stuff sports psychologists teach you, I don't really use them any more, but they are a huge part of boxing training for a lot of people.

I've always visualized myself winning. I've done it since I was really young, and it's not something I've ever been taught so I don't know where it came from. For instance, when I'm entering a big competition I'll see what looks like a photo of myself with my hand raised after winning a fight. Then it morphs into a movie of me being a champion.

As I mentioned before, even as a teenager I was so sure I was going to be world champion I felt exactly how it would feel and how I would react. I don't ever allow thoughts of losing to come into my head. I always believe that I'm going to win. I *know* that I'm going to win. There are never any 'what if's involved.

On the very rare occasion a negative thought tries to creep in I bat it away immediately. If there's even the tiniest hint of doubt, it's swiftly removed by a good training session. I don't ever set time aside to visualize, or make myself think about it constantly, it's just always there, naturally. I guess it's like a form of meditation in a way, but one that happens without me having to do anything. I do think if I ever lost confidence it would have a massive effect on how I box, and that's why I have to stay on top of my thoughts and work on that as much as I do my physical strength.

In my opinion, the key to success is being confident in yourself. I maintain my confidence by knowing that I've always done everything I need to do and I haven't cut any corners. Self-doubt creeps in when you don't do things exactly how you should and you try to take a shortcut. If you can go into a competition knowing you haven't left anything to chance, you don't have anything to be concerned about.

If you do cut corners, you may be able to fool someone else, but you can never fool yourself. As soon as you get into the ring, it becomes obvious to you, and very possibly your opponent, that you're not as prepared as you should be. Someone else can read that in your eyes the same way you're reading things in theirs.

I'm always working on improving. *Always*. After every competition, I take a step back and I look at how I approached things and how I can be better. There's a line in the book *The Art of War* by Sun Tzu that says, 'Know yourself to know your enemy,' and it's so true. The better you know yourself, the more capable you are of changing things you're not happy with. I know all of my faults, so I know how to change them.

When opponents watch videos of me boxing, even if it's only from the previous day, they're watching the past me and not me *now*. When I box them again they'll think they know my weak points but I'll already have spotted them myself and trained them out. By the time I take them on again I've improved on the flaws and I'll have totally changed the game, so they've got a whole new set of things to think about.

I'll have watched the same tape they've watched, so they're never one step ahead of me. If my hands have been too low at one point, they'll expect me to make that mistake again, but I won't. I'm very aware they'll be looking for weaknesses, but they won't find them.

Boxing is very much about intuition and mind games.

You're purposely trying to make your opponent make mistakes. Sometimes I'll look like I'm making little mistakes when, really, I'm aware of every tiny move I make. My opponent will think they're spotting a flaw in my performance but, in fact, they're falling into my trap. It's like the spider and the fly.

At the start of 2014, I found myself with another serious injury. I noticed that my left shoulder was really sore and I assumed it was just muscle pain from training. But when I got out of the ring after sparring one day it just didn't feel right and I could barely lift my arm. My doctor, Mike, booked me in for a scan, and when I got the results back it turned out I'd torn my rotator cuff and detached the top of my tricep from the shoulder. Mike told me there was no way I could rehab it back to health and that I would definitely need an operation. It was so disappointing to hear, because the Commonwealth Games was being staged in Glasgow that summer. It was the first time ever that women's boxing was going to feature and I desperately wanted to make history all over again.

I told Mike that I would book in for an operation as soon as I'd competed in the Commonwealths and the World Championships, and in the meantime I'd do some serious work to make sure my shoulder was in the best shape it could be under the circumstances.

Because I wouldn't have had the op by then, Mike had a meeting with the GB physios and they put a comprehensive structure in place for me to keep the pain at bay and allow me to train enough to be able to compete. Because I was in such extreme pain, I couldn't do more than four rounds of boxing at any time, and you can't usually do so little and expect to be ready for a major tournament, but it was my choice.

We broke my training up so I'd do four rounds of pad work in the morning and four rounds of sparring in the evening. Then I'd do my strength and conditioning. Because you have to use your shoulder a lot for running, I replaced that with cycling (which, to be honest, I wasn't that upset about).

I wasn't as confident going into the Commonwealth Games as I usually am with a big tournament, because I couldn't do as much as usual beforehand as I'd like to have done. The training was 100 per cent of what I was allowed to do but it wasn't 100 per cent of what a boxer would usually do before such a big event. I knew that I had to go into the Commonwealths being really tactical about what I did. My coaches and I tested out my strategy in a tournament called the Feliks Stamm in Warsaw, Poland. We wanted to see how well my shoulder reacted under pressure so we had an idea of what to expect later on. I was okay during the first bout, just a little bit sore, but during the second one I really felt it. By the time I got to the third bout, I was like, 'Okay, this is *really* painful now. This isn't good.'

Then came the fourth bout. I was in a really difficult position, because when you're boxing you want a punch to come as a surprise; people shouldn't be expecting it. But my arm was feeling so weak I had to put loads of effort into throwing a punch, so it was really obvious, which meant my opponents were forewarned. I had to be more tactical than ever and really think about when I threw my shots, and be certain that they were going to land. It was much more painful on my shoulder if I threw a punch with power and then missed, because it pulled on my joint.

I did win the tournament, but it wasn't easy by any means and because of that my coaches and I went back to the drawing board and had a rethink. We all knew I wouldn't be able to box to my full capacity if my shoulder hadn't improved before the Commonwealths.

I flew over to Glasgow in August 2014 feeling genuinely worried, which isn't like me at all. But I was still confident I could win. I'd faced enough difficulties before, and this was just one more obstacle I needed to overcome to prove to myself that nothing can keep me down. I pretty much had to box with one arm throughout the tournament and, of course, I couldn't let the organizers know I was in any pain or they wouldn't have let me fight. I was taking really powerful Ibuprofen to try and reduce the inflammation in my shoulder joint, and painkillers on top of that.

I was fighting against a girl called Mandy Bujold, from Canada, in the semi-final when I felt my shoulder go. It sounded like a firework going off in my head and I felt like the whole exhibition centre had probably heard it. One of my coaches shouted, 'Throw your jab!' and I was like, 'That's not going to work today. I can't do it!' I had to really work to beat Bujold, but I did.

I fought Michaela Walsh from Northern Ireland in the final. I lost the first round, and I felt annoyed because I would usually have beaten her quite easily. After that, I totally changed my tactics and started using my left hand as a backhand rather than as a jab. That way, I could disguise my left hand with my right hand. My right hand became a smokescreen and I'd wave that around in Walsh's face so she couldn't see my left hand coming, which meant I could score.

It was a tough match, but when the bell went at the end of the fourth round it was announced I'd won on a split decision, making me officially the first woman boxer ever to win a Commonwealth medal.

I don't know how many hours of rehab I did following the Games, but I know it was a hell of a lot. I was having rehab five times a day, including at weekends. I was doing a mixture of stretching, working with a Theraband and light weights. I still had the World Championships in Korea to get through, and things weren't looking good.

My mum was so worried about me she told me to get my shoulder sorted out rather than go to the World Championships. She's not the sort of person to blow things out of proportion but she was concerned it could get worse and cause lasting and irreparable damage.

I had a choice between taking part in the World Championships or getting my shoulder fixed and being able to compete in the European Games the following year. I followed my heart (and my mum's advice) and went ahead with the operation. I was terrified of my shoulder getting worse, so missing the Worlds was really my only option.

Because I missed the Worlds, I lost a lot of my ranking points, which in turn affected my seeding. If you're ranked number one, which I was at the time, when you go into a qualifier it makes it easier in that bracket. You get a bye in the first fight, which means you don't have to compete in the first round and you won't have to fight difficult people straight away. You generally won't get a tough opponent until you get into the quarter- or semi-finals.

On the one hand, I was gutted about having to take time out but, on the other, I was pleased that I got to spend a decent amount of time with my friends and family after working so hard for so long. I'd been training or taking part in tournaments non-stop for years and I think it was healthy to be able to take a step back and re-evaluate things and then go back into competing with renewed energy.

I had the operation ten days after the Commonwealth Games and I didn't go back into proper training until January 2015.

Ever since the operation, I've spent a lot of time strengthening my shoulder, and I've been lucky because

I haven't had any problems with it since. That shows how important it was to take that much time out. It may have felt frustrating at times but at least I didn't put my career at risk.

The workouts I do now vary but, generally, I do a little bit of work on my legs, and the majority of my workouts consist of things like press-ups, pull-ups and bench pulls. Pull-ups are one of my favourite exercises, which I don't think is something a lot of people say. I think it's because the more you do them, the better you get, and it's great to see how your body changes when you really put the work in.

The only thing I don't like doing are Russian leg curls. They're so painful on your hamstrings that when you get off the bench you can really feel it. It's a horrible exercise. It's important to keep my core very strong, so I do a lot of sit-ups and planks. Once your core is strong, you can work around it and master any exercise.

I find music really helps to keep me feeling energized when I'm in the gym. I listen to a lot of R&B, funky house, dance and hip-hop when I'm training. There are certain songs that mean a lot to me and, whenever I hear them, they take me back to the time when I listened to them a lot. For instance, Drake's 'Summer Sixteen' was the song that got me hyped up and ready for Rio, and Nicki Minaj's 'Moment 4 Life' is one of the motivational tracks that I often listen to before I get in the ring. The Chainsmokers' track 'Roses' was out when I met my girlfriend, and N-Trance's 'Set You Free' reminds me of my teenage years and going clubbing with my mates. It may come as a surprise, but I also love classical music. Disney is responsible for that. I used to watch *Fantasia* when I was a kid and that got me into it.

I have different playlists for different times. I normally update them every time a new song comes out I like and, when they get old or I get bored of them, I'll ditch them for newer ones. I'll listen to pretty much anything, apart from cheesy pop. You won't find me pounding the treadmill to One Direction any time soon.

It took me from January until July to feel ready for the European Games in Baku, Azerbaijan, and I had to work doubly hard at everything. I did a small tournament first, called Box Am, which acted as a good warm-up. It was nerve-wracking because you never really know how you'll perform after a long time out. You can feel good, but you don't know where you stand or what you need to work on until you compete for the first time. I knew I was ready to box again because I'd been through various tests to ensure I was fully healed. You're not allowed to box if you're not, because you'll probably do serious and lasting damage. I fought a girl who was the reigning European champion, and I won, so I went into the European Games feeling sharp and ready. It was the first time they'd ever done that sporting event and I created history yet again by winning a nice, shiny gold medal.

My training for 2016 was as intense as it had been for 2012. It was a long prep camp and, when we got to Brazil, I was totally buzzing to be taking part in another Olympics, but I was also excited about getting home afterwards, because I'd been away training at the English Institute of Sport in Sheffield for so long.

I was also nervous about how the Olympics would be handled. I'd only had experience of the London Games and they were structured incredibly well, but every time I read something about the Rio Olympics in the papers it all seemed to be doom and gloom. It you believe everything you read, the stadiums were half built and there were gangsters trying to take over proceedings. Then, of course, there was the big scandal about the Zika virus, which is a disease mainly spread by mosquitoes, and how dangerous it was. The Zika virus did concern me but, equally, I had to say to myself, 'If you want that gold medal, you've got to take your chances.' Having been out there, I don't think it was as bad as the media made out, and we took loads of precautions, like having plug-in mosquito repellents in the room. The organizers were also spraying the site with mosquito spray twice a day, and at five o'clock in the morning they would drop smoke bombs over the entire Olympic village to kill all the mosquitoes. It was quite dramatic, but also very safe. I didn't get bitten once while I was there.

I think it's a shame that the media tried to put such a negative spin on proceedings; it was totally fine once we were there. A lot of the stadiums weren't sold out and there weren't as many people as expected, but there was still a good atmosphere and we knew that millions of people back home were watching us on TV or keeping up with our progress on social media. It was so nice to hear from all the fans and we were all aware that the whole of the UK was behind us.

I didn't see any of the other venues, but I thought the boxing one was great, although it wasn't as well planned as London had been.

The accommodation reminded me of London because, again, it was like quite a basic student flat. There were some complaints the plumbing didn't work in some of the apartments and a lot of things had to be fixed while people were living in them, but before we arrived Team GB made sure everything was okay and working for us, so we didn't have any issues.

The catering wasn't on the same level as it was at the London Olympics – and food is, of course, very important to me – but we had plenty of places to eat and the GB team set up the British School, which was a place where only us Brits could go and get food whenever we liked. It was a nice place to hang out, so I ate there most of the time. The chefs were great and they'd make whatever you wanted.

As usual, everyone in Team GB massively supported each other. We had a tally chart of medals set up in the lobby of the GB accommodation block and it was amazing to see the chart going up and up. It was really motivating, and we'd all sit together in the communal area and watch how all the other athletes were doing on a big TV.

I mainly hung out with Joe Joyce and Savannah Marshall, because we'd trained together a lot. My general routine was to train, go back to the apartment for a sleep, go and eat, watch some TV, play my PlayStation and then go back to sleep. There wasn't much variety and there was quite a lot of waiting around. As with London, we weren't really allowed to leave the village unless we had permission. A lot of people were going to see the statue of *Christ the Redeemer*, but I'd already seen it so I was mainly hanging out in the apartment or going to the canteen to do lolly runs. They had these all-natural ice lollies that had bits of fruit in them in mango, coconut and orange flavours, and I got absolutely addicted to them. I was probably eating about six or seven of them every single day. I convinced myself that because they had fruit in them they were healthy. Obviously, the last thing you can do when you're due to compete is go partying, so having a lolly was about as exciting as things got while I waited for the boxing to start. The other athletes and I looked out for each other a lot in Rio, the same way we always do. Everybody tries to help each other out as much as possible. You're all aiming for the same goal, and that's to win, but it was four or five weeks before I had my first match. You're doing the same thing day in, day out, so you lose the buzz of being there.

If I had to do Rio over again, I wouldn't fly out until the week before I was due to compete. My competitions started a lot earlier in London, so I had something to occupy me, but I felt like I was in Rio for too long with not much to do.

By the time I started competing I was desperate to get into the ring, box, win my gold medal and go home and see my family. None of them flew over because it was such a long way and I would have worried about them being out there on their own. London had been so simple and straightforward, but this was a totally different set-up. Plus, Mum didn't want to have to leave our dogs. It was bad enough that I was away and they were missing me, so if Mum had gone away too they would have been lost.

I've got a Pomeranian called Bailey and a Doberman called Rio. They're amazing and they get on really well, but Rio's still a puppy so we have to separate them sometimes because he can be quite heavy-handed. Bailey isn't much taller than a can of drink and weighs a kilo and a half, whereas Rio is already massive and he bounds around trying to play with Bailey. I would say Bailey is the feistier one, though. He's totally fearless. In his mind, no dog is bigger than him. He's also very clever. If I'm competing and Mum's at home with him, she'll say, 'Nikki's on telly!' and he'll run up and sit down in front of the TV to watch me.

I was so excited when I got to Rio, but it slowly but surely turned into another training camp. I was counting down the days, hours, minutes and seconds until I could get into the ring and not have to train any more. Savannah, Joe and I were the last ones to compete and when we saw everyone else going to box we'd feel so envious. One of the male boxers, Joshua Buatsi, had already won a bronze medal, and we hadn't even made a start.

When my first match finally arrived I felt a little bit 'off' because I'd been there for so long, so it was quite tough. After that one I was fine and I got my flow back. Thankfully, I soon got into my stride and got my fire back and remembered that I'd gone there to do a job and not just to eat ice lollies. I'd gone to Rio to win, and it was gold or nothing for me. I wanted to be a double Olympic champion and nothing was going to stand in my way. Nobody likes coming second, but for me it's unthinkable.

My first match was in the quarter-finals against Tatyana Cobb of the Ukraine, and I felt more confident once that was over because I knew I'd got my first fight out of the way. The first match is usually the hardest for me, and then I pick up. I was disappointed with my performance overall, but I won, and I was happy that my Games had kicked off well.

I faced Cancan in the semi-finals next. I was nervous but I felt ready. I was focused and I knew I could beat her again. My nerves always turn into focus at some point, and that point is usually the second the bell rings. Something switches in me. It's like something takes over. I don't know if it's become second nature because I've done it so many times but my mind and body know it's time to fight.

Cancan had already told the press that she'd spent the last four years preparing and working out ways to beat me again another time. It was flattering that I'd been on her mind constantly since 2012. I'd have been the same if I'd won the silver and I'd had to spend those years listening to someone talking about their triumph. I'd have made it my life's mission to make sure I won the next time around. It's a long time to wait.

I knew how much she wanted to beat me. She'd changed things up to try and catch me out, but whatever it was didn't work because, unfortunately for her, she came up short again. Do I feel bad for her? *Sort* of. I understand that it must have been frustrating but, to be honest, I don't think she'd want my sympathy. She'd much rather have the opportunity to beat me again. And would she have felt for me if she'd won? Absolutely not.

I was excited about the final, against France's Sarah Ourahmoune. I'd beaten her four times before and I was confident that this match was going to go the same way. She definitely tried harder than she ever had done when we'd boxed before, and I don't know why that surprised me, because if you're in the Olympic finals, of course you're going to do everything you can to win. Other times when I've competed against her, she's lost heart halfway through the bout, but this time she put up a good fight the whole way through. Fair play to her. It was a good match and she was a really worthy opponent. I respected that Ourahmoune fought until the end. There wasn't any point where I was worried she might beat me, but I was quite taken aback because I was thinking, *Hang on, this is the moment where she's supposed to back down a bit, and she's not. She's here to really fight today!*

I take my hat off to her, because she made it a good fight and a show, but I knew I was going to win anyway. My technical ability was a bit in front of hers so I knew she shouldn't beat me.

I was on such a high in the moments before I won. I couldn't get complacent and I had to keep up my energy right until the last second, but I was on top of the world. All of those hours in the gym over the last four years had been worth every second of exhaustion. They'd all been for that moment.

My win was a unanimous points decision and I was awarded my second Olympic gold. The uproar in the stadium was ridiculous when I won. The crowd were going crazy. I stood there and took in the moment, knowing that I would never experience that feeling again. I was a double gold-winning Olympic champion and it felt *incredible*. I took a mental photograph to remember it by, and I couldn't stop smiling.

After doing some long interviews, I had to go into anti-doping. Although it took me four hours to wee again, it went by so quickly for a change because I was messaging everyone on my phone. Most of the people I would usually have spoken to about my win straight after the match were back home, so we were excitedly messaging back and forth. It's so strange, because everything is so silent while you're waiting (it's like being in a doctor's waiting room) and I wanted to scream at the top of my voice.

I celebrated my win by having a McDonald's. I *know*. I felt so tired after that I went straight to bed. I was like, 'I've done it. Now I want to *sleep*.' I'd been through so much to get to Rio and, actually, all I wanted to do was get some rest safe in the knowledge that I would be back in the UK within days.

It's pretty crazy that you wait four years for one tournament and then it's all over so quickly. I felt the pressure being lifted off my shoulders straight away. I had felt that need to win again every day for four years. Everyone had me down for winning gold, so I knew I had to do it. You have to want to be the best to be the best. And it feels very good if other people expect you to be the best too.

As with London, there was a lot of partying going on in Rio and everyone was having a great time. On the last day, everyone partied together, but I reined myself in because I knew that as soon as I landed back in the UK I'd have a ton of media to do and I couldn't handle the hangover. There are certain moments when you have to think, *It's just not worth how I'm going to feel in the morning*, and that was definitely one of them. I decided to stay in my room, talk to my girlfriend on the phone for ages and chill out.

I had a couple of drinks on the flight back; they were handing out loads of champagne. The entire flight was taken over by Olympians, so it was quite strange. It was a ten-and-a-half-hour flight and some people partied all the way home, so they were pretty much the worse for wear by the time we landed in London.

It was a fun journey, but the way the plane was set up was quite savage. The top gold medallists sat in first class and the ones who couldn't fit in first class were in business. If you'd won silver or bronze, you were in premium economy, and if you didn't win anything, you were in economy. I felt terrible for the people who were in the economy seats. It must have been a double blow to them. They didn't win a medal and they didn't get the nice seats. It was so harsh. I still can't believe the organizers did that. Mind you, if I'd known I was at risk of sitting in a cramped seat, it probably would have been another massive motivator for me to win.

All the gold-medal winners got together to do a selfie on the way back, and that was so much fun. We were all so excited to be going back home and we were going back with our heads held high.

We flew into Heathrow, and we got such an amazing reception. When the plane doors opened, there were so many media people and family members waiting for us on the concourse. We'd been pretty cut off while we were in Rio so we didn't know what the reaction would be like when we got home. I expected things to be exactly the same as when we'd left. We didn't really know what had been going on over here, and it was completely different from being in London in 2012, when you were in the middle of everything and you could gauge the public reaction. When we saw how happy people were with what we'd achieved, we were buzzing.

That was the first time I'd seen my family for weeks, and we hugged each other so tightly. I only got to see them for an hour and then I had back-to-back media for three days. I stayed in a nice hotel in central London, but I was horribly jetlagged so I barely got any sleep. I think I was on such a high the adrenaline got me through. I was appearing on breakfast TV and then going to radio stations and doing press interviews. It was a packed schedule and I drank a lot of Red Bull and coffee. I eventually finished doing interviews at 8 p.m. on the third day, and I went straight to bed. Next to winning another Olympic gold, it was the best feeling ever.

I enjoy doing interviews and meeting people, and it's actually quite easy. A lot of people get nervous, but I see it as having a nice chat with someone, and anything is easier than boxing. Nobody is trying to hit you in the face when you're sat in a TV studio, which is always a bonus.

I really like going on game shows, too, because, even though they're fun, there's also the competitive element. I did *All Star Family Fortunes*, which was brilliant, and I loved having my family involved. I made them all get into training by downloading the app on their phone so they could practise for weeks before. Yes, I was even desperate to win that. We were up against the former England cricket captain Michael Vaughan, and he was great, but we still won, which obviously made me very happy. And it made my family happy too, because they knew they would get an earful from me if we hadn't. I think it's fair to say I'm not just competitive about boxing. If you're going to compete for something, you may as well try to win.

Eight:

Homecoming Queen

The one thing that cast a bit of a shadow on the 2016 Olympics for me was the fact that some of Team GB's medical records were leaked. An online hacking group who called themselves 'The Fancy Bears' somehow managed to get hold of them and published them on their website, which meant they got picked up by all the papers.

Maybe I was naïve, but I didn't think that was something that could ever happen. I was really shocked at first but, because I didn't have anything to hide, I soon calmed down. I think I was more annoyed because it felt like an invasion of my privacy. It was my private information that was being shared with the world, and I was angry at the World Anti-doping Agency for letting it happen. There should be enough precautions in place to prevent leaks.

I found out my information was going to be released the day before it happened. Because I was forewarned, I was prepared, and I knew that the only things anyone could be at all interested in were my asthma pump and an allergic reaction I'd had to something a few years ago. It wasn't very exciting, to say the least.

I know that a lot of the other athletes came under scrutiny because some of the drugs they were using for certain conditions could be misconstrued, but they'd all been through really stringent checks. There could have been an athlete who was suffering from cancer, or HIV, and those are such personal things. How dare someone abuse that trust?

What people don't understand is that British athletes have all gone through the correct protocols to get the sanctions to use the drugs they need. Some people think it's the way forward for everyone who competes at a certain level to make their medical files public. Personally, I would have no problem with it at all, but it should be up to the individual.

What happened with the Russian doping scandal before Rio was even more shocking. The ones who ended up competing had to do special drug testing or have their previous samples looked at, and only athletes in certain sports were allowed to take part. I think it was the first time ever the Russian athletes' block was half full. There was room for another country to sit above them, and that's never happened before. It's not unusual for several smaller countries to share a block but, usually, Russia, GB, the US and China will fill an entire block by themselves.

We're tested constantly in the UK. You can be getting ready for a night out and, suddenly, there will be a knock on your door and an official is standing there ready to do a spot test. Testers are usually looking for blood doping, steroids or growth hormones. Basically, anything that could make you stronger or faster.

You're probably wondering how they know where you'll be and when, and the answer is that all Olympians have to fill out a form stating where you'll be for the next three months. If it changes, you can text or email to let them know officially, but they have to know for certain where you'll be for one hour of every day.

My life shifted so massively after 2012, but the change after 2016 was nowhere near as extreme. I think 2012 was the big game-changer, but by the time 2016 came around people already knew who I was, so things were much more sedate. I had loads of people coming up and congratulating me and asking me about the Games. They were patting me on the back and telling me how proud I'd made Britain.

I made sure I took a step back and acknowledged what I'd achieved, because it's easy to focus on the next thing and not enjoy your victory. The biggest moment for me was when I stood on the podium and realized I was the champion of the world. I was so overwhelmed I started crying. I didn't even cry after 2012, and at 2016 I shocked myself by how emotional I felt.

I went back to Leeds to take a break after I finished all my media commitments in London. I went out for dinner with my mum, brother and girlfriend to a Brazilian steakhouse in Leeds, and it was so nice to relax.

I went to both the Manchester and London Olympic homecoming parades, and I couldn't believe the turn-out, especially in Manchester, because it was pouring with rain. Over 100,000 people made the effort to come and see us, and I was blown away that they were prepared to stand in the rain to support us. That's when you know how much effect Team GB's medal success has had on the country. There's an amazing sense of pride and unity about the Olympics. When we get handed those medals we know we're doing it for our country.

It's become a bit of a joke in the press now that I keep my medals in a sock, but it's true. It's much easier to get them out than when they're in the presentation box. It's simpler to transport them, and they don't get scratched. It's the perfect home for them. I get asked to show my medals at pretty much every event or interview I go to, so I need a good way of carrying them around. When I'm at home I have them on display so that people can see them. People always want to at least have a look. Sometimes I wonder if people are coming round to see me or my medals. Everyone is always surprised by how heavy they are. They're really solid.

My mum always laughs because when I get home from a tournament because, no matter where or what it is, she always wants to see my medal. I'm pretty laid back about things – I'm more interested in having a sandwich and relaxing on the sofa than showing them to people. She usually ends up having to go into my bag to get it out herself because I'm too busy looking through the fridge for food. It's not that I'm not incredibly proud, because I am, but I get a bit embarrassed showing them off. But does it feel good when I hold my medals in my hand? I'm not going to lie: it feels *amazing*.

Because I took some time out after the 2016 Olympics and had a break from full-time training, I missed the European Women's Boxing Championships in Sofia, Bulgaria. But I had to give myself a break, because you're only as good as you're feeling, and I was pretty worn out. I felt like I'd done enough for that year and I was ready to re-evaluate again and consider my future.

Like most people, I think a lot about the future, and for me that means turning professional and acting alongside it. I love both of those things, and there's no reason I can't make it work. Mixed martial arts is a massive thing for boxers to go into now and there's a lot of money to be made from it, but I want to stick with boxing. It's what I know and love.

Professional boxing is very different from the way I've been competing so far; when you're pro, you're more in charge of your own life. You're in control of where your career is going and you get to decide when you're going to box and when you want to take time out. That would be perfect for me, because I would be able to decide when I'm going to compete and when I'm going to act.

Because I was a part of Team GB, they have had a lot of say over what I do and I was constantly in training. Obviously, I'm hugely grateful to them and all they've done for me – they've been there for me every step of the way, and they're incredible – but I feel like the time has come for me to have more say.

As a professional, I'll only be boxing the people in the pro ranks and I'll box up to ten two-minute rounds, whereas Team GB competitions comprise four two-minute rounds. I can train anywhere in the world I choose, but I'll probably do most of my fights in Britain and then go over to America to expand my horizons a bit. I could go somewhere with an amazing beach and sun and do the whole paradise thing but, honestly, I think I'd miss home too much.

The other big difference with going pro is that you get paid to box and you can make really good money. Now is the time when I want to set myself up for the future, so I have to start thinking about saving money and making plans.

It's a new era and a new beginning, and it's going to be so good. I'm really happy with the pro team, Frank Warren and BT Sport. I spoke to a few promoters and I felt like Frank Warren believed in my dream as much as I did, so I based my decision on that.

I think a lot of people were surprised: no one was

expecting me to sign with Frank, because of the stance he had taken on women's boxing in the past. He didn't used to be a fan, but when we spoke he said I'd changed his mind over the past eight years because he's seen how hard I've worked and how much I've achieved. He also told me that, every time he got in a taxi, he'd get asked about me more than any other boxer, and I think that says something.

It's nice to know I'm changing all kinds of people's perceptions about women's boxing and helping them to realize that women *can* box. I'm the first female who's ever signed with Frank. After I did, he said this about me:

> Of all the signings I have made in my thirty-five years in the sport of boxing, this is among the most I have been excited about. I think Nicola will be challenging for world titles within a year. We intend to lead her to become a multiple world champion. She possesses the talent and character to propel women's boxing to uncharted levels and help it to become a mainstream attraction. It is not all about gender, however; Nicola is simply a bloody good boxer whose presence on the card would enhance any fight night, and that is why we beat off considerable competition to be in position to showcase her on our shows.

That was pretty incredible to read. I was expecting a big reaction, but I wasn't expecting it to be as huge as it was. The announcement was massive on social media, and it was all over the news. The response I got was great. Everyone was really positive and looking forward to my pro debut. All the people who have followed me throughout everything have been saying how excited they are about me entering the professional game, and I feel exactly the same.

People will probably be wondering if I'm going to be competing at the Tokyo Olympics in 2020 but, sadly, it's probably not possible to do that *and* go pro, because I won't have the time to do both. So I've had to make a tough decision. And as hard as it's been, turning professional feels like it's the right next step for me, so I'll be focusing on that from now on.

Who knows? In a few years' time, I might change my mind and decide to take part in the Olympics again. I know it will probably be quite weird when it rolls around and I'll feel quite sad if I'm not a part of it. Mind you, I think Cancan will be pretty pleased if I decide not to compete at Tokyo. She'll probably be punching the air and thinking, *This is finally my moment!*

I've always been fearless about trying new things. I can make decisions very easily, and I've got better and better at that as I've got older. I'll listen to other people's advice but sometimes I don't know why, because I already know the answer. It's so important to listen to yourself and to trust yourself. There's no harm in getting other people's opinions, but don't let anyone tell you what to do, put you down or tell you something isn't possible. Persevere – keep trying. I wouldn't be where I was if I didn't have self-belief and trust.

Also, it's always been important to choose my role models really well. Karren Brady, who is the vice-chairman of West Ham FC and appears on *The Apprentice*, is a massive one for me. She's been working in what is considered to be a 'man's world' for so long and she's never thought twice about going for what she wants. She's achieved so much. I was invited to go for dinner with her once and she was so inspirational. She told me she admired what I've done with my career and we talked about how she's survived – and, in my opinion, excelled – in a very male-dominated environment. She knew she had to work twice as hard as some men do, and she did. There are still a lot of women struggling with the same kind of thing, and it's a case of being strong and knowing that you're inspiring other women.

I'm looking forward to new challenges, to breaking new barriers and creating a new path for women to follow in boxing. A path has been carved out in amateur boxing, and now it's time to do it in the professional world. I love the idea of getting back to what I enjoy doing, which is breaking down walls. There's huge potential in the professional game and they're just waiting for someone to walk in there and open things up. I think, in a couple of years, we could be seeing a woman headlining in Vegas, and I'd love that to be me. It's amazing that the professional promoters believe in my dream and think it's possible. And I know I'll have the full backing of my incredible family.

I'm also thinking about the outfits I can have designed, which is one of my big priorities. I like the fact I'll be able to come up with an idea and have Swarovski crystals and different types of leather and silk, so I'm genuinely excited about that side of it, too. I can really express myself and look the part. At the moment, I'm very restricted with what I wear – only whatever the Team GB kit is that year. If I'm on TV in front of millions of people I want to be wearing something that reflects who I am. So, from a style point of view, going pro will be great.

The only downside with going pro is that I'll have to pay for everything myself, such as physios, doctors, training and coaches, which will be totally different from being on Team GB, where everything was taken care of. I'll also have to be more self-motivated than ever, because I won't have someone kicking me up the backside and making me train constantly. And the way I'll do that is the way I always have, by focusing on what I want to achieve. I'll always have that desire to win, and that won't change when I go pro. I want to be a world champion pro one day.

I'm ready, and this is about taking my career to a

whole new level. With a good team behind me, we can make women's boxing something really special. Having the right team around you is so important. I've been very lucky with the amazing people I've worked with, and I hope I can continue working with some of them in the future. I'll miss them very much.

There were also rumours that I was going to do *I'm a Celebrity . . . Get Me Out Of Here!* last year. They weren't true, but I would like to do it. I think, of all the reality shows, it's the one that I'd enjoy most. I'd love the challenges because, obviously, I'm really up for anything that pushes me.

As for the acting side of things? I really want to play strong characters like the ones Kristen Stewart, Angelina Jolie and Jennifer Lawrence play. Something like *The Hunger Games* would be perfect for me, and my ultimate dream would be to play a female James Bond-type character. I'd also love to play a detective. I love *24* with Jack Bauer, and I also love *The Walking Dead*.

As well as going pro and acting (because I won't be busy enough!), I'd love to do some sports commentating one day, so I've added that to my list of plans. I also hope to get married and have some kids and have a happy ending to go with all of my other happy endings. That's definitely a plan. There's no reason why I can't have a family and still box. Mary Kom won a world title after having twins. She's just had another child and is still coming back into the sport. It's not a case of doing one or the other.

My girlfriend is the most incredible woman I've ever met. I'm usually pretty laid back when I meet people I like but with her I was rendered speechless. I'm very open about being bisexual, but when I started doing interviews back in the early days of my career I never knew what to say about my sexuality. I didn't think it was something I needed to talk about, because it had nothing to do with my boxing. And no one ever asked, so I didn't mention it. I certainly wasn't hiding anything, because that's not something I would do, but I didn't want to randomly offer up the information.

I don't want people to think I'm ashamed of being bisexual, because that's the last thing I feel, and when I was eventually asked about it outright I was honest. It wasn't that I was living in fear of someone 'exposing' me because, quite frankly, what's the big deal? If some people have a problem with it – and let's remember, we're not living in the fifties now – that's up to them. I have the attitude that people either like me or they don't, and I honestly don't mind either way. All I can do is be myself. How can you be anything else?

When I think back now, I think I always knew I was bisexual but I didn't understand it properly until I was older. There were certain girls I really liked but I couldn't explain why I felt the way I did about them.

I was attracted to women but I figured it was because I thought they were cool or I wanted to be friends with them. I didn't realize at that time that it could mean something more.

I 'officially' came out when I was fifteen, and I told my mum first. I was so nervous, because I didn't know how she would react. What would she say? Was she going to shout? Would she be shocked? I went into the conversation preparing for the worst. We were both standing in the kitchen, and I said, 'Mum, I need to tell you something. I'm bisexual.' And she very casually said, 'Oh, that's okay, I kind of knew anyway. Do you mind putting the kettle on?' Her reaction was amazing. My mum is very understanding and kind, but I'd built the conversation up so much in my head I had put a lot of expectation on how she would feel. But it was like I'd just told her I wanted a pizza for dinner. My brother reacted in a similar way to my mum. He just shrugged, as if he was wondering why I was bothering to tell him.

Like most people, I first started dating in my teens. I had crushes when I was young, especially on Eva Longoria, but it wasn't until I was sixteen that I started going on dates. I was always pretty confident about dating and meeting people when I was out with my mates, but I didn't have my first serious relationship until I was eighteen, with a girl I met in a club in London. I thought it was a really serious relationship, and we were together for two years on and off, but in the end I realized it wasn't right.

I didn't get into a relationship for another couple of years but, since then, I've pretty much always been with someone. I'm not someone who *needs* to be in a relationship and, looking back, I can see that some of the people I was with weren't right for me and that maybe I should have waited. It was often other people putting pressure on me to make something casual into a proper relationship and I'd often agree to make things easier.

I have dated guys, and I like rough-and-ready types. I'm not into pretty model types at all. I don't tend to fancy the guys you're supposed to but, having said that, Brad Pitt is amazing in *Snatch* and *Fight Club*.

It was a great achievement to top the 2012 *Independent on Sunday* Pink list of the most powerful LGBT people. That was a great feeling – to think that I'd beaten people like Jessie J to the top. I've always been very supportive of LGBT issues. I've also won a couple of *Attitude* awards, and I've been interviewed for *Attitude* and *Diva* magazines. I'd like to do more LGBT stuff, but it's hard finding time in my schedule at the moment. I love going to the Pride marches. For some reason, there's something really special about the one held in Brighton.

There were forty-four openly gay athletes competing at the Rio Olympics, and I think it's brilliant that, like me, those gay or bisexual people felt like they could be open. But, equally, I do think, *Who cares? Does it have to be such a big issue?* The press ran loads of reports about it and made out it was such a big deal, but it did make me think, *There are no articles about how many straight people there are.* If people want to be out, that's great, but if they don't, I understand that too. There shouldn't be any pressure.

If you think about how many athletes there were in Rio – over 11,000 – I'm sure it's likely there were more gay athletes than those forty-four, but they chose to keep their private life private. And I respect that as much as I do the people who were out. It's their business and it doesn't make a difference to their performance. Being gay or straight didn't help anyone to win a medal.

I'm lucky, because I've always felt very comfortable with myself. I know some kids have trouble with coming out and being able to talk about things with their parents. I also think there are so many more places both kids and adults can get advice and support these days, which is amazing.

My idea of a perfect date is something out of the ordinary. It can be anything from indoor sky diving to going to a pool hall. I love active dates like go-karting and Laser Quest, because I think you find out so much about someone's personality and who they really are. You're not going to find out a lot about a person on a date at the cinema.

My girlfriend Marlen is also a boxer and competes for the US. I first met her way back in 2009 when we moved into the same boxing weight class. She had always been 48 kg and I was 54 kg, and when women's boxing became an Olympic sport we both moved to 51 kg. We knew of each other, but we didn't chat or anything because we spent most of our time with our respective teams.

She's the opposite of me because, when she walks into the gym, she doesn't chat or have a laugh, whereas I'm always having fun. Marlen always says she thinks people assume she's mean, but she only has training on her mind when she's in the zone. I guess, because we're so different, we didn't really hit it off, even though I did think she was incredible looking from day one.

We fought a lot of the same people from 2009 onwards but, for some reason, we never came face to face with each other. Then, at the end of 2015, Marlen and I were at the same training camp in Colorado. She was one of the first people I saw when I arrived; she was walking down the corridor of the venue with one of her friends. She was saying hi to everyone around her and when she said hello to me I had this really weird reaction. I was trying to fix my broken pass for the Olympic training centre and when she spoke to me I panicked and didn't say hello back. I'm usually so confident around people but, when I opened my mouth, nothing came out. In my head, I was going, *Say hi! Say hi!*, and it was so awkward I walked away.

I saw her again in the dining room that night and she

came over to chat to my team but, again, I was dumb-struck. I was looking everywhere but at her, and I think the one word I said throughout the entire conversation was 'snowboarding'. She looked at me like I was crazy.

A few days later, Marlen was in the gym with a mutual friend of ours called Cam F. Awesome (I know, it's an amazing name). He'd asked me to go out for dinner that night, and when he asked Marlen if she wanted to join us she was like, 'Are you kidding? I can't go out with her. She doesn't even talk!' Cam did his best to convince her that I was pretty chatty once you got to know me and, in the end, she decided to give me the benefit of the doubt.

Because Cam is a vegan we went to a local vegan restaurant, but because I was so wrapped up in Marlen I didn't even notice. I ordered one of my favourite things from the menu: nachos. When our meals arrived we all tucked in, but all of a sudden I started to feel really odd. I felt really unwell and I suspected it was a nut-allergy reaction. I asked Cam and Marlen if there were any nuts in my meal and Marlen dropped the bombshell that the vegan 'cheese' on top of my nachos was made of cashew nuts.

I explained I was seriously allergic to nuts, and Marlen started panicking. She asked me if I needed to go to hospital and, because I was trying to play it cool, I said really calmly, 'Yes, I think so.' I was genuinely trying to style it out, which is ridiculous. You can't style out a nut allergy. My throat was starting to close up and I was finding it hard to breathe.

I think Marlen and Cam thought they'd nearly killed me. They drove me straight to the hospital. I was probably quite close to going into shock but instead of thinking, *Oh my god!* I was thinking, *Marlen is really concerned about me. Maybe that means she really likes me?* In reality, at that point, she was probably thinking, *I don't want this girl to die.*

As soon as we got to hospital I got an epinephrine injection and, thankfully, I started to feel better straight away. I knew I would be fine once I was treated, because I've had reactions before, but it wasn't until the swelling started to go down that I knew for sure I'd be okay. Marlen and I ended up chatting for ages while we were waiting in the hospital, and I think she was shocked by how much I talked – she finally got a glimpse of the real me. That was a good chance for me to show her that I wasn't weird and that I can form whole sentences. It wasn't the most fun night of my life, because of the whole hospital drama, but it's one I'll never forget because it was when things started to click between Marlen and me.

Because it was such a crazy night, Marlen and I really bonded, so from then we started hanging out every day. Every free minute we had we were together, and the only time we weren't was when we were eating, because we had to eat with our teams. Slowly but surely, over the course of the camp, we ended up getting together.

I hated saying goodbye to Marlen but, a few weeks later, I flew to America to see her. I had my qualifiers for the Olympics coming up and we did some training together, and then she flew to England to spend time with me. Things took off really quickly after that.

In fact, things took off so quickly that, shortly before Christmas, I proposed. I'd known for a while I wanted to do it, but I kept it completely secret from everyone and I had the ring designed and made so everything was ready. We stayed in the Shangri La Hotel at the Shard in London, and I proposed over dinner in our hotel room. I was so nervous but, thankfully, she said yes, and it was one of the best moments ever. It was so nice, because the room's got a 180-degree view so you can see right out across London. It was so beautiful. We haven't made any wedding plans yet because we've both got so much going on, but when the time's right we'll start making decisions on when and where it's going to be.

A lot of Marlen's friends were really surprised when we first got together because she'd only ever had boyfriends before we started dating. I was her first girlfriend, and I think it came as a bit of a shock to her too. We both expected to be fighting each other at some point, not dating each other.

Luckily, Marlen has got tough skin and, like me, she's

not the kind of person who worries about what other people think. She's been really open with her friends and family and they've completely accepted that we're together.

It's not always an easy relationship, because we're in different countries, and in the beginning I wasn't sure if it could be anything long term, considering the circumstances. But we make it work. We commute back and forth across the Atlantic to see each other, which is taking a long-distance relationship to the extreme.

Marlen is also planning to go pro soon and that should mean that we can spend a lot more time together, because we'll have a lot more control over what we do and when. Thankfully, because we're no longer in the same weight class there's no chance of us ever fighting each other in the future. That would be *very* weird.

It is hard at times, because there's more interest in my love life now I'm dating another high-profile athlete. I think, when you're in the public eye, you can still choose how much you want to share about yourself to a certain extent, but it's still going to be trickier if both people are well known. I didn't ever hide the fact I was dating another athlete, but I didn't shout it from the rooftops either. If I was ever asked about my love life, I would admit I was with someone, but I didn't share too much. In the end, people worked it out for themselves.

It just works between Marlen and me. I've never got

on with anyone as well as I do with her, and she's un-believable. You know when you see those cheesy rom-coms where people completely adore each other, and you think, *That'll never happen. That's not real. There's no way anyone can actually love someone that much?* I actually *have* found someone I love that much.

Nine:

Future Proof

One of the most important things for me, no matter what I do in the future, is that I continue to inspire other women. Growing up, I didn't have many female role models, apart from my mum, and sadly, there weren't any Olympic women boxers for me to look up to. It was still considered a really strange thing for women to do and I do wish I'd had a strong female in that field to look up to so I could follow her lead. That's why it feels so amazing to me to be able to be a role model for young women now. It's so important to see the next generation coming through, and to see them competing and doing well. I really hope young women look at me and feel inspired. I've had some amazing feedback from girls who have said on Twitter and Instagram that they've wanted to get into boxing or another sport, or even just to work harder in life, because of what I've achieved. I was at an event recently and this guy came up to me and said that his daughter had been doing ballet for years but, when she saw me box, she told him she wanted to do that instead. I was really taken aback and I thought, *You go, girl!*

It's amazing to think that just by doing what I love doing I'm helping other people to do what they want too. That little girl probably didn't have anyone else to guide her before. I didn't ever set out to be a role model, but it's an amazing by-product of what I do.

I know that my hometown of Leeds is incredibly proud of me. After I won gold in London in 2012 they painted two of the postboxes on Cookridge Street in Leeds city centre gold in tribute (I got two because one of them is for business post and the other one is for residential post, and it didn't look right only having one painted, so I lucked out). Nestled in between the two postboxes is my commemorative paving stone, which I was given after I won my MOBO award. I went along with Kanya King, the founder of the MOBOs, and I laid the stone myself. It says on it, 'Tell me I can't and that's why I will', which is one of my mottos for life. It makes me feel so proud, because Leeds is where I made myself a champion. I've decided that the street the postboxes and paving stone are on should be called 'Nicola Adams Way'. I am joking. *Sort* of.

More women than ever are doing sport now. The last major survey showed that 7.21 million women play sport regularly, which is 250,000 more than it was two years ago. And the gap between the amount of men and women doing sport has decreased from 2 million to 1.5 million in that time. Officials think a big part of that change is down to 2012 and 2016, and it's great to be a part of that.

After I won my medal in 2012, there was a 50 per cent increase in women regularly taking part in boxing, and I hope all of the female athletes that have been successful make it ten times easier for other women to walk through that world. There's a lot of good talent coming through. We're getting medals at the Europeans and Worlds from the juniors and the youth, so it feels like a great time for British boxing. We need to support them because we need more women to take over from me when I retire.

There are so many women doing boxing for fitness too. Apparently, a lot of the Victoria's Secret models do it to stay in shape. It's definitely become a lot more popular and it is an incredible full-body workout.

I'm sure people think that, because I'm a boxer, I don't enjoy dressing up and putting on make-up and doing my hair, but I do. I love all of that stuff, and being a boxer doesn't mean you can't be feminine. I think people tend to pigeonhole women who box and think that you can't be strong *and* enjoy wearing nice clothes.

I am extremely pro-women, and it's funny because I didn't used to want to call myself a feminist because, if I'm being really honest, I had a skewed idea of what that was. I thought if you called yourself a feminist it meant you were anti-men and you were really angry about everything. I'm sure feminists were portrayed that way to stop women from uniting and making themselves heard. It wasn't until I googled 'feminism' that I realized it was just someone who wants equality for both the sexes. And who doesn't want that? I've been trying to make women's boxing on an equal par with men's for the past twenty years, and I'll carry on for another twenty years and beyond.

Everyone should be equal. Women should earn the same as men and be able to do the same jobs. If someone is right for a job, it shouldn't matter what sex they are. It's a shame that women feel that they have to fight to be equal to men, because they already are. *Enough now!*

It's amazing for me to look back and see how far not only I've come, but how far women's boxing has too. I feel so grateful for everything, and I'm excited about what's next for me. It's incredible to think that I've set records that can never be taken away from me. That really means the world to me. Whatever everyone else does, I'll always be the first. I love that, and I massively appreciate everything I've had along the way, in good times and bad, and the people who have been there for me.

Sometimes I'll stop and have a moment where I stop and think about the fact that I'm a world champion and I can't stop smiling. As of 27 May 2016 I was the reigning Olympic, World, Commonwealth and European champion at flyweight, and my achievements are mine. For ever.

I used to watch my hero Ali saying, 'I'm the greatest!' and now I can say that too. I'm where I want to be and I'm everything I want to be.

Ten:

Life Since Going Pro

The last year has been a really big and very exciting one for me. So much changed when I turned pro. I moved countries, got a new trainer and took part in my first pro fights, which went even better than I could have hoped. (Well, most of them…)

Things went brilliantly in the lead-up to my first professional fight at the Manchester Arena in March 2017. It was something I'd been working towards for some time and, when it came around, I was ready.

It was quite intense media-wise and there was a lot of focus on me because it was the first professional match I'd ever taken part in and people were interested to see how I'd do. I felt like all eyes were on me, but I also got an amazing amount of support from people on social media. And, of course, my family were right behind me.

I trained a lot beforehand, and I felt like I was in a good place when it came to my fitness. My regime was kind of similar to how it had always been, but because there are such big differences between fighting as a pro and as an amateur – in pro fights, there are no head guards, the gloves are a different size and there are different rules – I did have to mix things up a bit. So it was a bit of a learning curve. I didn't realize just how different it would be, going from the amateurs to the pros, and I've learned a lot.

I was more nervous than usual in the days running up to my first fight because I wanted to perform well and prove to people that I'd made the right move. There was also the whole thing of not knowing what to expect. I wasn't sure if I would feel different, or if the crowd would react differently to me.

I still play on my Xbox before I fight because I find it so relaxing, and I played it that morning to take my mind off things. I know it may seem weird, but it does help.

Competing as a pro is less about the volume of punches I throw and more about placing them correctly. In amateur fights you throw a lot more punches, but in the pros every punch has got to land right. I've kept my speed, but there's more power behind my punches and every one is precisely thought out. This was the first time I was going to be using the new techniques I'd been working on with my trainers. (We'll come to that later.)

Once I got into the ring, I realized it felt the same as my previous fights, so my confidence came flooding back. I was already thinking, *I'm going to win this*. I never allow any doubt to creep in. If you think you're going to lose, you've already lost.

It helped that I felt great in what I was wearing. My kit was designed by a lady called Sophie, who is brilliant. She used to design the women's gymnastics team's kit and she also designs for a lot of male boxers. She's great at putting sequences together, so I basically told her that my colours were going to be black, white and gold, and I asked her to do something cool with them. She took my sizes, got to work, and that was it. I was so happy with the result. I wore white-and-black shorts with 'Lioness' written on the back in gold. The Lioness tag came about when I turned pro. It started because, in a way, I've always been the leader of the pack. My mum says it's also because I roar. She calls herself Mamma Lioness.

After having to wear the Team GB kit for so many years it was nice to have the freedom to express myself. I've got a lot more individuality in what I wear now, and I don't have to be the same as everyone else, which definitely has a knock-on effect to how I'm feeling when I compete. If you look good, you feel good, and I love going into the ring wearing something that truly reflects my personality.

I fought Virginia Carcamo from Argentina and I won with forty points to her thirty-six during four two-minute rounds. It felt amazing when the bell went and I knew I'd been victorious. The crowd went absolutely mad and I was on top of the world. All the hard work I'd put in had paid off. My family and I went for dinner at Fazenda in Manchester afterwards to celebrate, and we were all buzzing after my win. They'd been as nervous as me, so it meant a lot to them that it went so well.

Once I had that first pro match out of the way, I felt like I got back into my comfort zone, and I was so ready for my next one. It honestly couldn't have come soon enough for me. Especially as I was going to be fighting in my home town.

The next fight was at the First Direct Arena in Leeds, and it was just as incredible as the first. Steve Franks, my first trainer, came over from Ireland as a surprise, and it was so good to see him. The reception I got was unbelievable. It was like I was fighting for a world title. I'd been dreaming about that moment for a long time, and to walk in to hear the crowd chanting 'Yorkshire' was an incredible feeling. I wanted to do well for the supporters, and they were so excited there was no way I was going to let them down.

I fought Maryan Salazar from Mexico in that match. Mexicans are known for being tough and strong, but I stopped her after thirty-five seconds of the third three-minute round. The three-minute rounds suited me more than the two-minute ones. The two-minute rounds are too much of a rush and I don't really have any time to do anything, whereas with the three-minute rounds I can keep relaxed and get my punches right. They will definitely be my preference, going forward.

A lot of my friends came along to that match so we all went out clubbing afterwards. We had an area of a club sectioned off so we could hang out and catch up and it was the perfect way to wind down after such an uplifting evening. I had a few drinks, so lunch with my family at the Leeds branch of Fazenda the following day acted as a bit of a hangover cure. We had a really good meal and it made me realize how much I miss my family now I'm living in America.

I started going back and forth to San Francisco a lot in early 2017 when I found the coach I really wanted to work with as a pro. I'd tried out different coaches in the UK and I wanted to try some in the US as well. I met with a few great ones and, in the end, I decided to go with a guy called Virgil Hunter because he's such a good, solid coach. He took Andre Ward, who is also a former gold medallist, and made him into a powerful pro champion. He also trains Amir Khan and he's got an incredible reputation. I couldn't imagine a better person to be with.

He already had a full team before I came along and he admitted that, at first, he wasn't sure if he could take someone else on. But apparently something about the way I looked at him convinced him he needed to work with me. It must have been the steely determination in my eyes!

I eventually moved to San Francisco so I could work with Virgil full time and, although England will always be my home, I do feel pretty settled in America now. You really get the most out of training when you're somewhere where it's sunny all the time because it means I can work out outside a lot, whether it's swimming, running or boxing.

Virgil isn't super-strict, like people would expect him to be. In fact, he's pretty calm. But he's a very technical and precise trainer. In that way, he reminds me of Alwyn Belcher, and I took to him straightaway because of that. He'll make me do certain moves numerous times, until they're perfect. There's no let-up, and that's what I love. He wants to be the best, and so do I. He introduced me to some new moves and body shots and taught me how to create power from your feet and how to turn properly, and it's changed the way I box.

I train five times a week now, with Wednesdays and Sundays off. On the days I train I work out twice a day, doing strength and conditioning or swimming or running in the morning, and then boxing in the afternoon. I usually work out at around 8 a.m. or 9 a.m., and then the next session will be around 3 p.m. Each session is about an hour and a half so I have plenty of time to rest in between.

Yoga has also become a regular part of my training now, and it's a lot harder than I expected. I always thought it would be gentle, but I do struggle to hold the poses and it takes a lot of effort. I struggled to touch my toes when I first started because I'm not at all flexible, but I have got better, and I'm improving steadily. We do hot yoga, which is pretty hardcore, and I sweat a lot. I think, when it comes to exercise, we're all good at different things. It's important to find your strengths and not dwell on the things you're not so good at.

Like anyone, I have days when I'm tired and I may not do as well during training as I'd like to, but I still do it. As long as you don't make excuses and think, *Ahhh, I'll go tomorrow*, you'll be okay. Showing up is the main thing. If you don't, it's a slippery slope and, before you know it, you've had a week off . . . and a week can easily turn into a month.

Sometimes I wake up and think I don't want to go and run around a track, but I always find the motivation.

The only time I take time off from my regime is if I'm ill, but since I've been living in California I haven't been unwell once. A big part of that is down to what I eat. I still get all my meals delivered, so all the work is done for me and I don't have to worry about the calorie, protein and carb content. They're all nutritionally balanced and I know I'm getting everything I need. I can't see myself learning to cook anytime soon. I know I should, but it's *so* much easier having someone else make the food for me. Making a meal feels like a lot of work if you're going to eat it in minutes.

I stick to a healthy diet most of the time, but ice cream is my go-to treat if I want to indulge. I have to be careful, because I can go through a big tub on my own. I go to a local restaurant in San Francisco where they serve massive portions of ice cream in waffle bowls and I can easily eat two large ones, so I stay away from there!

I still weigh myself every day to stay on track, because it is easy to slip, and you don't want to go too far in the wrong direction. If I do notice a bit of weight going on,

I pull things back and I up my exercise. And I put down the ice cream.

I'm really enjoying living in San Francisco and I would honestly say that, aside from the weather, it's not that different to the UK. People are people wherever you are. I'm in constant contact with friends and family back home. My brother comes out during the school holidays, so we still get to spend a lot of time together, and I like to get back to the UK around once a month for a week or so to catch up with everyone. Especially my mum.

One of the worst things that's ever happened to me was finding out that my mum had been diagnosed with breast cancer, in May of last year. It came as such a shock. As everyone knows, my mum means everything to me and I was terrified I would lose her. She discovered it by chance one day when she was taking her bra off. She felt a small lump about the size of a peanut, and she said that she just knew something wasn't right. She went to see her doctor and was referred to hospital for tests.

My mum, being my mum, didn't tell my brother and I at that point because she didn't want to worry us if there was nothing wrong with her. I was training for a fight in Vegas and she said later that didn't want to take my focus away from that. Every time I spoke to her, though, I sensed that something was wrong. I even asked her outright what was going on, but she tried to play it down. One night I phoned her and said to her, 'I know you're not all right, Mum.'

It was a horrible shock when she finally told me the truth. I knew something had been going on with her and that she was hiding something from me, but I had no idea it was something that serious. I was devastated, but I told her that, whatever happened, we would all get through it together.

Because she was referred for an emergency appointment my mum was seen at the hospital within two weeks. She had to have a mammogram and a biopsy. Her partner, David, who she got together with last year, went into the room with her when she had the biopsy and he found it so overwhelming he almost passed out. He started sweating and he had to be taken out of the room and given a chair, some water and some biscuits, and an ice pack for his head. My mum laughs and says she was thinking, *Hang on, aren't I supposed to be the patient here?*

When the results came back and confirmed it was breast cancer, Mum said that, even though she kind of knew, nothing could have prepared her for the terrible news. She burst into tears and the first thing she thought was, *How long have I got to live?*

She had an operation to take out the tissue surrounding the cancer and three of her lymph nodes at the beginning of August. Two of the nodes were clear and one of them had a tiny amount of cancer in it. Thankfully, she didn't have to have chemotherapy, but she had to have radiotherapy every day for three weeks. Everyone rallied around her. I had just bought a new house back home, next door to where I used to live with my brother. The sale went through a week before Mum had her operation, so the timing was perfect because it meant she had somewhere to convalesce. Also, my brother was still next door so he could check up on her and help her out.

I flew back from America to spend some time with my mum, and it was so hard because I hated seeing her going through so much. I don't mind someone punching me square in the face, but I can't stand to see my mum in pain. She is such a strong woman but, understandably, it knocked her for six. I arranged for Soul Mates food to deliver meals to her every day while she was having radiotherapy so she was getting proper nutrients into her body and she didn't have to worry about cooking.

I had to go back to America because I had some long-standing commitments, and I hated having to leave. I knew Kurtis was going to keep an eye on her at all times and I phoned her at least once every day. David was also an amazing support for her, as were his parents.

Following the radiotherapy, Mum had to go for a bone scan to make sure her bones hadn't been affected. Then she was put on hormone tablets, as well as some other medications.

She's doing really well now. She does get tired, but she looks after herself and sleeps if she needs to. It's only been recently that we can talk about the cancer openly, because it was too hard to speak about but, now we can all see how well she's doing, it makes it easier.

I really want to help fundraise for breast-cancer charities in the future. I've already done some work with them in the past but it's very important for me to get more involved and do what I can to help.

In the end, my big Vegas fight didn't take place. I was supposed to fight in September 2017 in the undercard (the boxing match before the main event) for the GGG versus Canelo fight.

Vegas has been my dream for so long and I was so excited about boxing there. But my opponent, Alexandra Vlajk, failed the medical tests so it got cancelled minutes before we were due in the ring.

I was in the dressing room of the T-Mobile Arena in Vegas at 2 p.m., putting my shoes on ready to go out, when I got the news, and it was gutting. I'd been working on some new things I wanted to showcase in the fight so it was a massive disappointment for that reason as well.

My third and final match of 2017 took place in Canada in mid-December. It felt different because it was my first pro match abroad. It was also *so* cold. It was minus 30°C at night and, one day, when I tried to go shopping, I had to give up and go back to the hotel after ten minutes. I had my Canada Goose jacket on and I was still freezing. After that, the only time I went outside was when I travelled from the hotel to the venue. I admire the people who live there because they just get on with it, but I would be terrible living with those brutal temperatures all the time.

The fight itself was great. I got my second stoppage, which is where the referee makes the decision to end the match early, and I felt comfortable with it. It all came together, and my coach was impressed, which was the main thing. Billy Joe Saunders was also fighting, so some of the lads I train with back home were there, and it was nice to see them. I also wore another great outfit, which had a breast-cancer symbol on it in honour of my mum. I dedicated that match to her and I wanted to win it for her. I'm so happy I did.

After a very difficult year for the family it was lovely for us to be able to spend Christmas together at my new house. Now I'm away so much, it means a lot to us to be together.

We played Monopoly after our Christmas dinner but, because of how competitive we all are, we ended up playing until around 3 a.m. None of us wanted to go to bed because we didn't want to lose. At one point I could see that Mum was tired and needed a lie-down but even she refused to give up. That was a sure sign she was getting better.

Bailey came to live with me in San Francisco for a while, but I took him back with me at Christmas and my mum wanted to keep him for a little while. He's had to have an operation to remove a load of his baby teeth, which he wasn't happy about, but he's still as feisty as ever. Rio is back home with my mum too. He's way too big to come and stay in our apartment. He would take up half of it! But I still get to see him when I go home.

I've got another dog in America, a French bulldog called Ollie who has bright blue eyes. He was a nightmare when he was a puppy because he thought everything was a chew toy. Anything he could get his teeth into, from cables to trainers, he did. We had to be so careful about what we left around the house and so much stuff got destroyed but, thankfully, he's come out of that phase now.

As you may already know, Marlen and I split up earlier this year, but I'm now refocusing my energies on to all the things I have coming up, and on achieving a world title.

Now I only have to compete once every couple of months my life isn't as full on as it was. Because of that I get a lot more time off in between fights so I've been able to go and see the sights of San Francisco. I'm also doing things with friends and family that I wouldn't have been able to in the past, like going to christenings and weddings. I've been able to spend quality time with people and it's so nice to be able to do 'normal' stuff again.

I even went on a proper holiday. I know! I went to Cabo, in Mexico, and I promised myself that I would turn off my phone while I was were there and not reply to emails, texts or phone calls. And believe it or not, I did. It was very hard at first because we're all so used to having our phones with us twenty-four hours a day, and it was so weird because I couldn't look anything up online or see who had contacted me. But once I got used to it I totally relaxed and enjoyed myself. I even wanted to stay in Cabo longer, which is unheard of for me, because I'm usually itching to get back home after a holiday.

I didn't turn my phone back on until I left the hotel and, when I did, it didn't stop pinging. It took me forever to reply to everyone. To be honest, I felt like I needed another holiday afterwards.

I've also had time to work on other projects, and the one I've enjoyed most is my clothing range for Everlast, which is stocked in Selfridges. Loving fashion as much as I do, it was a perfect thing for me to do.

I'd been in talks with Everlast for a little while, because they really liked my lion logo, and then they asked me if I was interested in bringing out my own clothing range. I already had it in my head that I'd like to do something like that, and it was such a brilliant opportunity. Selfridges is so iconic, and every fashion brand going is trying to get their foot in the door and be stocked in there, so I felt very flattered. Vogue did a piece on the range too, which was wicked.

I had a lot of input with the designs and materials. It was important to me to be really involved, so that was something I made sure would happen very early on. Needless to say, I've got a lot of the range myself. I love the T-shirts with the big lion logo on the back, and I love the snapbacks because they've got a leather peak and they look so cool. Hopefully, I'll be able to do more of the same in the future too, because it's something I feel proud of.

Another very exciting thing that's happened to me recently is having a Barbie made of me for International Women's Day. It looks like me and it's got the same haircut and it's wearing my pro boxing outfit. It looks legit. I really hope it inspires other girls to do whatever they want to and to break boundaries. I'm the first ever boxer Barbie, which feels very special.

I went to the Barbie headquarters in LA in February and I got to go on a tour and see what goes into creating a Barbie, and it's so much more than I expected. When I first saw the doll, it was weird. Imagine coming face to face with a very realistic but very tiny version of yourself. It was crazy.

As well as all of that, I've got some more exciting things in the pipeline. I swear, just when I think I can't do any more, I find a way to do something else. My schedule for the next year is as mad as ever, so my life is mapped for the foreseeable future.

I've still got a lot of goals. As well as staying at the top of my game, I want to carry on working on my fashion range. And I would still love to have kids one day.

I also like the idea of working with up-and-coming female boxers in the future. It would nice to still be in touch with the amateur side and help the girls who are breaking through. Women's boxing is doing better than ever at the moment. It's getting a lot of coverage and it's really good to see. Us girls are taking over.

Eleven:

How to Train like a Boxer

Nicola's strength and conditioning coach, Andrew Wiel, explains what it's like to train pro boxers, and gives his top tips for aspiring boxers.

What are basics of boxing training?

Boxing training is very different from the kind of training the average person does to lose weight or get stronger. Boxing training is about speed, endurance and strength. You can't be too much of one thing and not enough of another. You can't have a primary physical focus; you need to be a good all-rounder.

Certain sports have specific coaches, so Nicola has her boxing coach, Virgil, who teaches her how to box well. Where I come in is making sure that her body is *prepared* to box well. If her boxing coach comes to me and says, 'Nikki's jab is kind of slow right now so can you work on some hand speed,' I do that. Or if she's losing a bit of endurance at the end of a round, we'll work on building up her stamina.

As a boxer, you have to be very focused and disciplined. Strength and conditioning is a more generalized aspect of fitness, and you do a lot of that with combat sports, because it's essential for agility and speed. When you do the more specific boxing training you're actually trying to hurt one another, so there's a lot of injury prevention involved in strength and conditioning as well.

If someone came to me and said they wanted to become a boxer even though they've never trained for it before, the first thing I would do is footwork drills and coordination, because they're just as important as punching accurately. You need to make sure your whole body is in the right position before you throw or dodge a punch. In addition to foot coordination, I would incorporate core stability, hip stability and knee and ankle stability to make sure their body is going to be ready for the thudding that's going to happen if they start sparring.

Yoga may not be the first thing you think about a boxer doing, but there are so many different types of yoga and they are all good for different things. Yoga is great for flexibility, and that's so important for boxers. The hardest thing about yoga is breathing, and once people learn to breathe well yoga starts being much more effective and efficient. Bikram yoga is more strength-based than some other types, so that's what boxers tend to do most.

Cardio is also very important, but you can't just be able to run a long way or do quick sprints. You have to be able to do both. Interval training is fantastic for helping you build both speed and endurance.

General strength is also essential because, in boxing, you can't be strong physically in just one area. It's no good if you have big muscly arms and weak legs. You need to have strong legs and strong abs, and a strong back and a strong neck. You need to be solid and firm.

It's not just about whether you can throw a powerful punch.

How does injury prevention work?

With Nikki, we *have* to focus a lot on injury prevention before we can do speed or strength work. All exercises have risks and dangers and the possibility that you will get injured, so you want to prepare the body and make sure the exercise isn't going to harm the person in any way and that they don't have an imbalance somewhere in their body that could potentially cause issues.

All boxers use their shoulders a lot when fighting so they need to do exercises that help them build strength there. I first check in with them to see if their shoulders have been bothering them at all. Then I'll choose a mobility or stability exercise for the shoulders, depending on the athlete's needs, to do both before and in between each set of exercises. Push-ups are great for this.

Core, hip and knee strength are also really important, because any imbalance or instability there can cause problems in the lower back. If you look at anyone when they're standing still, generally one hip will be higher than the other. While it's normal for most people, it can be a real problem for boxers. Doing exercises on just one side of the body can help to address this, but there's a lot more to it than that. It's not something that can be fixed just by doing exercises at the gym. The athlete needs to be consciously thinking about how they are sitting and standing all the time and must be able to adjust their body accordingly. It takes a lot of sustained effort and energy.

Do you use different techniques to train men and women?

When it comes to training, everything comes into play, from weight to gender to age. Wear and tear is going to take its toll, so older boxers may be more prone to injuries. I often get asked if it's different training men and women, and it's not that the boxing itself is different, it's the fact that men and women are built differently so they're at risk from different injuries.

Women generally have wider hips than men, and men usually have broader shoulders, and that means they have different needs. They will be more at risk of being injured in some areas, and they may be stronger in others. With women, because their hips tend to be wider, their knees are often internally rotated and therefore more prone to injury. Women are also often more flexible than men, which is good, because stiffness can cause injury as well as negatively impacting on performance. But there is also such a thing as being too flexible – you need an element of stiffness for stability.

What about the differences between training amateurs and pros?

There are definitely differences here as well.

Because amateurs might have four or five fights in one weekend, they have to be constantly aware of their weight. If they gain too much muscle, they'll be overweight for their category and that obviously impacts on the training they do.

A pro may only fight four times a year so, most of the time, their weight doesn't matter too much. It's much more about training for specific events rather than maintaining one weight all year round.

Luckily, Nikki and I are very similar in terms of our personalities and we're both happy-go-lucky, but when it's time to work out, it's head down, let's go.

She's very coachable and I don't ever have to explain things repeatedly. I've worked with other really high-calibre athletes where I have to go into lots of detail about how they're supposed to be doing a certain move. With Nikki it comes very naturally and she gets things so quickly. She is very in tune with her body and where she should be in a space. She's instinctive, and that's one of her biggest assets.

How can people stay motivated when training?

Everybody has those days when they turn up to train and they're tired and not really in the mood for it. What differentiates the exceptional athletes from the average ones is that they understand that those days are the most important. Knowing that, no matter how they feel mentally, they can still push themselves through is what gives them the edge in a fight.

If someone turns up to a training session and they're tired, I have a spiel I give to them. I'll say, 'I'm not here to be your cheerleader, that's not my style. But if you can train today, you'll be able to do it next time as well. We're here, let's make the most of it.'

Being an athlete is all about practice. You have to practise how to push yourself when you're tired and not feeling like it. Like everything, it gets easier if you practise getting through it over and over again.

Acknowledgements

To all the strong, ambitious women who never knew weakness, and those who choose not to live by it, to my mother who showed me no fear, to my brother who has always shown me love, to my friends, family and supporters who have shown me no doubt and to my team at ROAR Global. This one's for all of you.

Special thanks also goes to my very first coach, Steven Franks, who always respected me as a female boxer; and to both Rob McCracken and Dr Mike Loosemore who nurtured me through many personal highs and lows in my amateur career with Team GB.

To my lifelong trainer, Alwyn Belcher: my success wouldn't have been possible without you. I would not be the person I am today without your belief and advice. I can never repay you, but I will always try.

Thank you.